Glass Working

EDITED BY
PAUL N. HASLUCK

**Fredonia Books
Amsterdam, The Netherlands**

Glass Working

Edited by
Paul N. Hasluck

ISBN: 1-4101-0614-4

Copyright © 2004 by Fredonia Books

Reprinted from the 1899 edition

Fredonia Books
Amsterdam, The Netherlands
http://www.fredoniabooks.com

All rights reserved, including the right to reproduce this book, or portions thereof, in any form.

In order to make original editions of historical works available to scholars at an economical price, this facsimile of the original edition of 1899 is reproduced from the best available copy and has been digitally enhanced to improve legibility, but the text remains unaltered to retain historical authenticity.

PREFACE.

THIS Handbook contains, in a form convenient for everyday use, a comprehensive digest of the information on Working Glass by heat and by abrasion, scattered over ten thousand columns of WORK—the weekly journal it is my fortune to edit—and supplies concise instruction on the general principles of the subjects on which it treats.

In preparing for publication in book form the mass of relevant matter contained in the volumes of WORK, much that was tautological in character had to be rejected. The remainder necessarily had to be arranged anew, altered, and largely re-written. From these causes the contributions of many are so blended that the writings of individuals cannot be distinguished for acknowledgment.

Readers who may desire additional information respecting special details of the matters dealt with in this Handbook, or instruction on kindred subjects, should address a question to WORK, so that it may be answered in the columns of that journal.

P. N. HASLUCK.

La Belle Sauvage, London.
　November, 1899.

CONTENTS.

CHAP.		PAGE
I.	Appliances used in Glass Blowing	9
II.	Manipulating Glass Tubing	26
III.	Blowing Bulbs and Flasks	49
IV.	Jointing Tubes to Bulbs, etc.; Forming Thistle Funnels	65
V.	Blowing and Etching Fancy Glass Articles; Gilding and Embossing Sheet Glass	81
VI.	Utilising Broken Glass Apparatus; Boring and Riveting Glass	97
VII.	Hand-working of Telescope Specula	113
VIII.	Turning, Chipping, and Grinding Glass	141
IX.	The Manufacture of Glass	150

LIST OF ILLUSTRATIONS.

FIG.		PAGE
1.	Black's Blowpipe	10
2.	Support for Blowpipe.	10
3–5.	Spirit Blowpipe and Reservoir	11
6–8.	Blowing Arrangements	12, 13
9–11.	Stand Blowpipe	14, 16
12.	Glass Blower's Table	17
13–16.	Foot Blowers	18, 19
17–21.	Bunsen Burners	20–23
22.	Directed Flame of Burner	23
23–26.	Spirit Lamps	24
27.	Sections of Glass Tubing	26
28.	Sections of Glass Rods	27
29.	Triangular Tool	27
30.	Charcoal Cones	27
31–33.	Blowpipe Flames	27, 28
34.	Method of Severing Glass Tube	29
35.	Method of Bending Glass Tube	29
36–41.	Forms of Bent Tubes	30–32
42.	Barometer Tube	32
43–48.	U-shaped Tubes	32–34
49.	Method of Heating Tube	34
50, 51.	Method of Drawing Tube	35
52.	Method of Sealing Tube	35
53.	Method of Drawing Glass Tubes	36
54.	Method of Slanting Tube in Frame	37
55, 56.	Sealed Tubes	37
57, 58.	Glass Rods	38
59.	Barometer Float	38
60, 61.	Finishing Mouth of Tube	40
62.	Drawn Tube	41
63–65.	Method of Jointing Tubes	41
66.	Drawn Tube for making Pipette	42
67–76.	Making Pipette	42–44
77–85.	Method of Jointing Tubes	45, 46
86.	Glass Blowing on Large Scale	47
87–92.	Bulb Tubes	50
93–104.	Making Flasks	51–53
105–107.	Making Bulb Pipette	53–55
108.	Badly made Bulb	56
109.	Bulb Tubes	56
110–116.	Making Bulb on Centre of Tube	56–58
117–121.	Blowing several Bulbs on one Tube	59, 60
122–127.	Liebig's Potash Bulbs	60, 61
128–130.	Making Oval Bulb	62
131–137.	Making Flask with Side Tube	63, 64
138–152.	Method of Sealing Tubes to Bulbs	65–69
153–165.	Making Filter Pump	70–73
166–171.	Making Eudiometer	74
172–175.	Method of Making Thistle Funnel	75
176.	Foot and Stem of Wine Glass	76
177.	Modified Tool	76
178, 179.	Wine Glasses	76
180–185.	Test Glasses	76
186–188.	Making Funnel	77
189, 190.	Thistle Funnels	77
191–203.	Funnels	78, 79
204–215.	Making Glass Pipe	81–83
216–219.	Making Glass Cigarette-holder	84
220–223.	Gallenkamp's Vacuum Tubes	85, 86
224.	Steam Dipping Vat	87
225.	Ladle	87
226.	Drainer	87
227.	Pencil Stick	88
228, 229.	Stilettoes	88
230.	Pouncing Pin	88
231.	Gutta-percha Bottle	88
232, 233.	Gutta-percha Acid-vats	88
234.	Rest for Arm	89
235, 236.	Perforated Design	90
237.	Badly Etched Design	92
238, 239.	Unfinished Etching on Glass	94
240.	Etched Glass	94
241.	Cracked Test-tube	97
242.	Test-tube with Re-made Mouth	97
243.	Method of Cutting Wide Test-tube	98
244.	Method of Cutting Glass Bottle	98
245.	Broken Test-tube	99

FIG.	PAGE
246.—Method of Re-sealing Test-tube	99
247.—Cracked Flask	99
248.—Flask mended at Neck	99
249.—Dish made from Flask	99
250.—Cracked Beaker	100
251.—Beaker re-made	100
252.—Retort cut for Dishes	100
253, 254.—Adapter	101
255.—Improvised Retort and Receiver	101
256.—Thistle Funnels made from Retort Neck and Pipette	102
257.—Jar made from Bottle	103
258.—Deflagrating Jar	103
259.—Copper Tube for Boring Glass	103
260.—Boring Holes in Glass	104
261.—Drill Stock for Glass	106
262.—Diamond Drill Bit	108
263.—Plate Drilled for Riveting	109
264.—Drill with Tape Twisted	110
265.—Nippers for Bending Wire	111
266.—Convex Tool	113
267.—Hone squares Tool	114
268.—Glass Discs together	115
269.—Overhanging Glass Discs	115
270.—Curved Section of Glass Discs	115
271.—Working Speculum over Tool	116
272.—Edging Glass Disc in Lathe	117
273.—Radius Bar on Wall	118
274.—Convex Metal Curve-gauge	119
275.—Concave Metal Curve-gauge	119
276, 277.—Diagrams showing Paths of Speculum	123
278.—Facets of Pitch on Glass Surface	126
279.—Faceted Glass Tool	127
280.—Tool for Faceting	128
281.—Lamp and Blade for Foucault Test	131
282.—Foucault Speculum Test	132
283.—Shadow with Shutter inside Focus	133
284.—Shadow with Shutter outside Focus	133
285.—Shadow with Shutter at Focus of Special Mirror	134
286.—Oblate Spheroid	134
287.—Spere	135
288.—Hyperbola	136
289.—Long Focus Parabola	136
290.—Short Focus Parabola	136
291.—Speculum in Silvering Bath	137
292.—Chuck for Holding Glass	142
293.—Section of Chuck	143
294.—Diamond Point Turning Tools	144
295.—Lens in Lathe Chuck	145
296.—Shanks for Nibbling Lenses	148
297.—Nibbling Lens with Shanks	148
298.—Grinding Spectacle Lens	149
299.—Edge of Lens after Grinding	149
300.—Spectacle Lens in Frame	149

GLASS WORKING.

CHAPTER I.

APPLIANCES USED IN GLASS BLOWING.

GLASS is worked in one of two ways—either heat is applied to soften the glass, which is then moulded or blown to shape; or the glass is reduced by an abrasive process in which emery or similar material suitably lubricated is employed. To those two methods perhaps another can be added—that of etching with acid; this, however, has its application principally in the decoration of the glass articles produced by the method first noted. It is intended to devote the early chapters of this handbook to information on glass blowing so far as it pertains to the manufacture of the smaller glass fancy articles, chemical apparatus, etc.; glass etching and embossing will then be considered, and this will be followed by a description of the processes of shaping glass by abrasion.

Heating appliances at the service of those who wish to make a practical acquaintance with the art of glass blowing are four in number. They comprise the ordinary gas jet, various forms of blowpipes, the Bunsen burner, and the spirit lamp. The first of these, with which a great deal of work can be done, requires no description.

The blowpipes used in glass blowing are of two kinds—"mouth" and "foot." These are subdivided into (1) those held in the hand, and (2) those supported on a stand. The simplest form of blowpipe to hold in the hand is the mouth blowpipe.

Black's form of mouth blowpipe is shown by Fig. 1. Particles of saliva may be spurted out from the ordinary mouth blowpipe, but in Black's form the saliva is held at the bottom of the conical tube. Glass tubes canno be bent satisfactorily in the mouth blowpipe flame, as being finely pointed, its heat is too concentrated. It is, however, very useful for making small bulb-tubes.

A support for the blowpipe while in use, which will leave the hands free, may easily be made from a small slab of wood having fixed in it a wire; this has a loop at the end, in which the nozzle tube of the blowpipe may rest (Fig. 2).

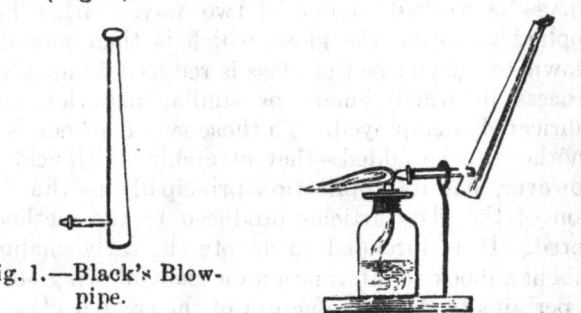

Fig. 1.—Black's Blowpipe.

Fig. 2.—Support for Blowpipe.

At Figs. 3 and 4 is seen a blowpipe which, though very useful, is not so good as a gas blowpipe. It consists essentially of two parts—the blowpipe proper and a receptacle for spirit. The materials required are— one piece of brass tube, ½ in. diameter, 4 in. long; one piece of tube, ¼ in. diameter, 8½ in. long; and one piece $\frac{3}{16}$ in. diameter, 2 in. long; a small piece of stem of clay tobacco pipe, piece of wick about 1 in. or 1¼ in. wide, and a brass cap with a female screw upon it. A thread for the brass cap to screw upon is first cut upon one end of the ½-inch tube. A ¼-in. hole is drilled in the cap, and the ¼-in. tube pushed through and soldered, so that 3½ in. of it penetrates into the outer tube when the cap is screwed on.

A hole is drilled and tapped in the ½-in. tube, for

the $\frac{3}{16}$-in. tube, at about 1 in. from the end. The small tube is now screwed in, and any projecting portion inside the larger tube is filed down.

A piece of the tobacco pipe, $\frac{3}{4}$ in. long, which is intended for the jet is broken off by means of pliers,

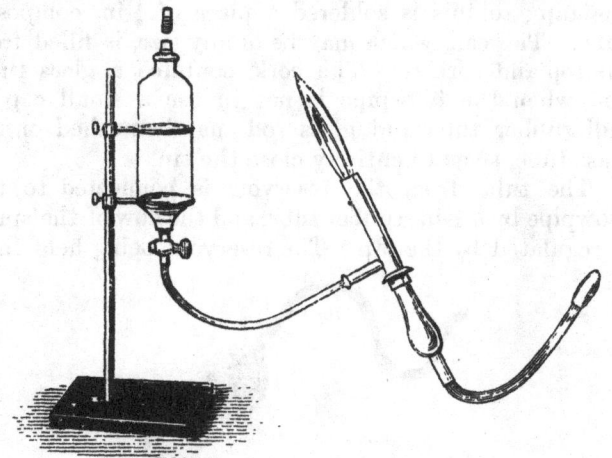

Fig. 3.—Spirit Blowpipe and Reservoir.

and half its length is filed down until it will go inside the $\frac{1}{4}$-in. tube (see Fig. 5).

A piece of wick, a trifle over 4 in. long, is rolled up so that it will go inside the outer tube, and the inner tube is pushed inside the wick and screwed in place, care being taken that the nozzle is concentric with the outer

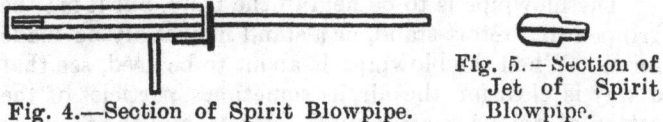

Fig. 4.—Section of Spirit Blowpipe.

Fig. 5.—Section of Jet of Spirit Blowpipe.

tube. The wick should just appear at the mouth of the blowpipe, and any excess may be cut off before commencing work.

For hand use the air tube may be $8\frac{1}{2}$ in. long, and for convenience of holding, a bradawl handle may be bored right through and glued upon the tube, leaving about 1 in. of the latter out for connection to the air supply.

It is necessary that the supply of spirit should be apart from the blowpipe. The reservoir, Fig. 3, is a tin can, in the bottom of which is soldered an ordinary gas tap; to this is soldered a piece of $\frac{1}{8}$-in. composite tube. The can, which may be of any size, is filled from the top and corked. The cork contains a glass tube, and when the blowpipe is not in use a small cap of indiarubber tube and glass rod may be pushed on the glass tube, so as to entirely close the tin.

The tube from the reservoir is connected to the blowpipe by a $\frac{1}{4}$-in rubber tube, and the flow of the spirit is regulated by the tap. The reservoir, being held in a

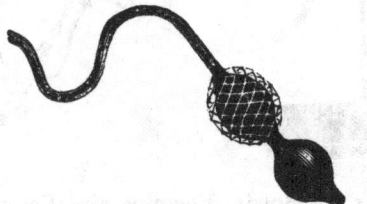

Fig. 6.—Simple Blower.

ring of the retort stand, is raised or lowered until the level of the liquid is about the same as the mouth of the blowpipe, so as to ensure a regular supply without overflow. If this is attended to, the wick will last for a considerable time.

The blowpipe is to be held in the hand, but it may be gripped to a retort-stand, or a stand may easily be made for it. When the blowpipe is about to be used, see that a way is clear for the air, as sometimes particles of the cotton of the wick cover up the nozzle, and the flame is blown about in a very unsteady manner.

Petroleum spirit or benzoline (not paraffin), costing about 6d. per pint, is the best for this blowpipe; it gives a smoky flame very suitable for the purpose, and during blowing a flame $4\frac{1}{2}$ in. long may be obtained; whereas with methylated spirit the flame is only $3\frac{1}{2}$ in. long.

APPLIANCES USED IN GLASS BLOWING. 13

The blowing arrangement for this blowpipe (Fig. 6) consists of two indiarubber balls, connected together by rubber tube. Air enters by an opening in the end ball, but owing to a valve it has to escape by the rubber tube; thus pressure on this end ball inflates the middle ball, which is made of elastic indiarubber, and a constant blast of air is kept up.

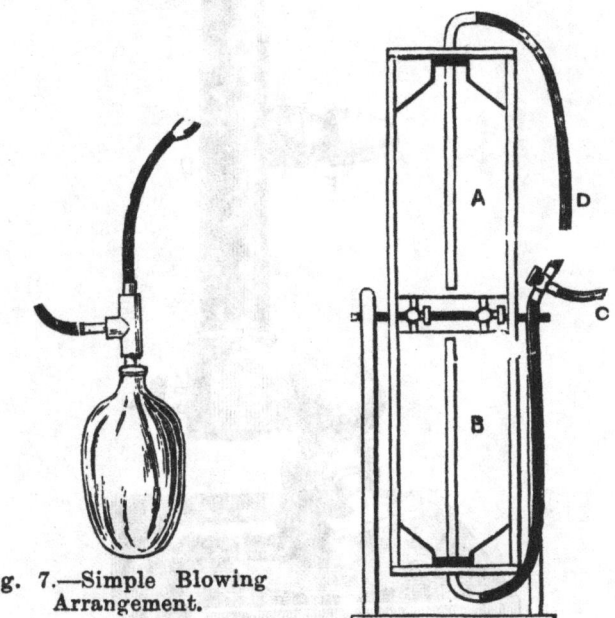

Fig. 7.—Simple Blowing Arrangement.

Fig. 8.—Hydraulic Blowing Arrangement.

Another useful blowing apparatus (Fig. 7) consists of a brass T-tube, communicating at one opening with a bladder, whilst to the other openings indiarubber tubes are attached, leading respectively to the air jet and to a mouthpiece. A fairly strong flame may be obtained without much exertion by screwing the T-tube to a bench. If this is done in such a manner that, when seated, the bladder may be gripped by the knees, then, whilst still blowing into the mouthpiece, the flame may be further urged by increasing the pressure on the bladder.

The hydraulic blowing arrangement (Fig. 8) is very useful, but more work is required in making it. A and B are gallon size oil-cans, with their bottoms connected

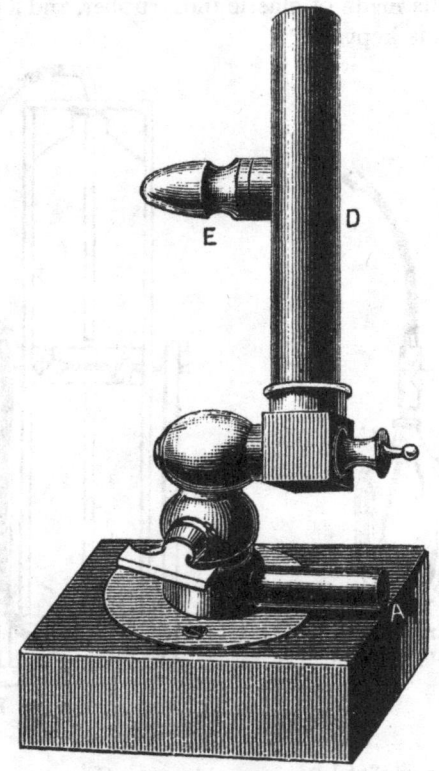

Fig. 9.—Stand Blowpipe.

by two brass tubes, each having a tap. At the mouth end of each can is a lead tube, which is bent round as shown in Fig. 8, to receive the end of a rubber tube. The two cans are securely fixed together by a framework of wood, through which passes a round bar, acting as a pivot. A stand for this has a thick wooden base and two uprights having a hole bored in each, in which the pivot works. At C, Fig. 8, near the top of one of the uprights, is shown a tap, and an indiarubber tube is connected from the lead tube in the lower can to this tap, and this is connected to the blowpipe. In operation the apparatus may be used with either can uppermost; the air for the

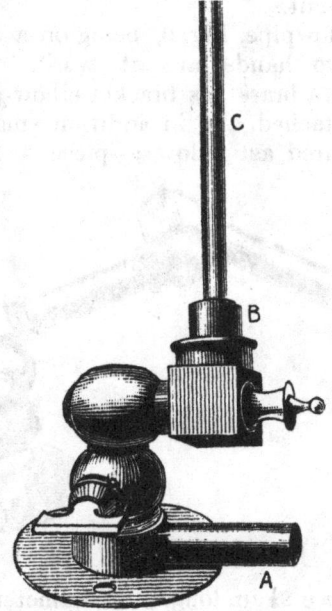

Fig. 10.—Stand Blowpipe showing Inner Air-tube.

blowpipe always issues from the lower can, from which it is expelled by the pressure of the water which runs from the upper can.

To set the apparatus working, fill one of the cans with water and turn it so that the full can is uppermost, taking care to have both connecting taps turned off. When the cans are secure in position, as shown in Fig. 8, turn the tap on the tube C so as to connect the lower can and the blowpipe. The rubber tube D from the upper can is left open to the air. To get a blast of air through the blowpipe connected on to c, turn the taps to connect the reservoirs: if a moderate blast is required, open only one tap, but for a full blast open both of them. When the water has run from the upper can, turn off the taps and reverse the apparatus, which delivers one gallon of air each time—a considerable amount.

The gas blowpipe, Fig. 9, being on a stand, is useful when the two hands are at work. The requisite materials are a brass gas bracket elbow-joint, with tap and flange attached, and in addition small brass tubes will be required as follows:—piece 4 in. long, ½ in.

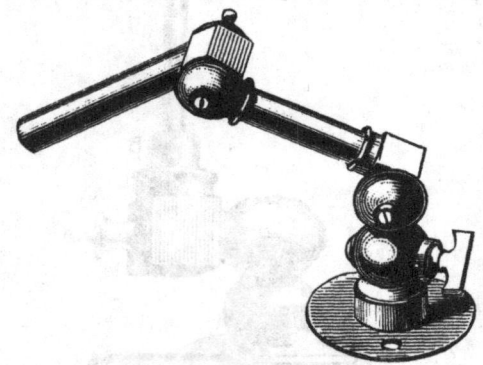

Fig. 11.—Blowpipe with Double Joint.

diameter; piece 2¼ in. long, ⅜ in. diameter, threaded on one end; piece ¾ in. long, ⅜ in. diameter; ½ in. long, ⅜ in. diameter, threaded on each end; 3⅝ in. long, ¼ in. diameter; brass nozzle 1½ in. long, with ⅜ in. thread cut inside one end; a small piece of sheet brass, and a block of wood for the blowpipe to stand upon.

Commence by drilling a hole in the brass between the flange and the cock, and at right angles to the latter; tap it for a ⅜ in. tube. The air is to come in here, and the gas by the side tube E. Cut a circle of brass ½ in. in diameter, and solder it over the hole at back of flange. Screw in the bit of tube ¾ in. long at B (Fig. 10), cut a piece of sheet brass 1⅜ in. long, ½ in. wide, coil it into the form of a ring, and solder it as shown at B ; at the same time solder it inside the ¼ in. tube, C, and file the outside of B until tube D will slip on with a push.

Now take tube D and in the side bore a hole ⅜ in. in diameter at the middle of the tube ; file the end of the nozzle, E, to a hollow curve, so as to fit close against the tube, D. Screw into the nozzle a bit of ⅜ in. tube, and file it hollow in the same way until about one-sixteenth of an inch projects ; knock it into the hole in tube D, and solder. Push the tube D on to B, and see that the inner tube C reaches to within about ⅜ in. of the end of tube D. Bore a hole in the wooden block for the brass flange to

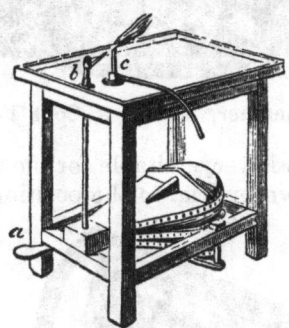

Fig. 12.—Glass Blower's Table.

enter, and thus leave the flange flush ; screw it to the block and screw in the side tube A.

The gas is let in at E ; there will always be a tap on the gas supply with which to regulate it, and the air is regulated by the tap near the flange. When the gas supply is a long distance off, and alternating heats are required, put a tap on E.

With this blowpipe (Fig. 9) only one movement of the elbow-piece is obtained ; but if another tube and elbow-joint are inserted between the burner and the stand, a very useful double vertical motion will be got (Fig. 11). This will higher the blowpipe, and allow the flame to be directed downwards.

The bellows may be double action, such as those made

by Fletcher, Russell & Co., or a pair of ordinary bellows fitted to the bench (Fig. 12). The foot bellows illus-

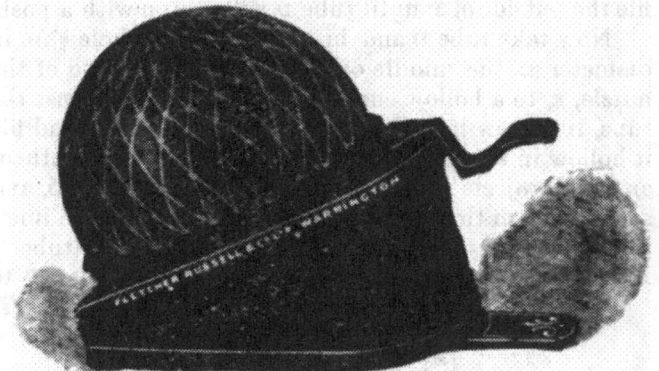

Fig. 13.—Fletcher, Russell & Co.'s Foot Blower.

trated by Fig. 13 is very suitable for blowpipe work. In the bellows shown by Fig. 14 the position of the blower

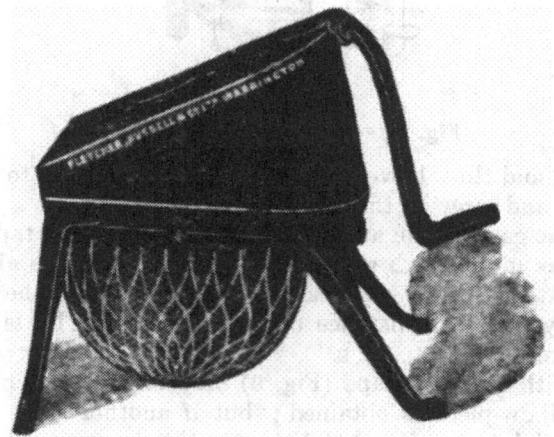

Fig. 14.—Fletcher, Russell & Co.'s Foot Blower.

is reversed, and risk of injury to the rubber disc is thus avoided. In Fig. 15 is seen a spring reservoir in place of the indiarubber disc. In the cheaper form shown by

Fig. 16 the reservoir may be hung up on the wall out of harm's way.

Fig. 15.—Fletcher, Russell & Co.'s Foot Blower.

The Bunsen burner—known to some as the atmospheric burner—was invented by the late chemist of that name. It burns with a blue flame when properly

Fig. 16.—Griffin's Special Foot Blower.

adjusted, gives out great heat, but practically no light; and when a cold body is brought into the flame it does not deposit soot.

20   GLASS WORKING.

Improved forms of Bunsen burners are illustrated by Figs. 17 and 18 ; Fig. 19 shows an ordinary home-made one. There are holes at the base of the upright tube, through which air is drawn by the gas as it ascends the tube. Fig. 20 shows the base of the burner with the tube unscrewed, to show the small nipple through which the gas issues.

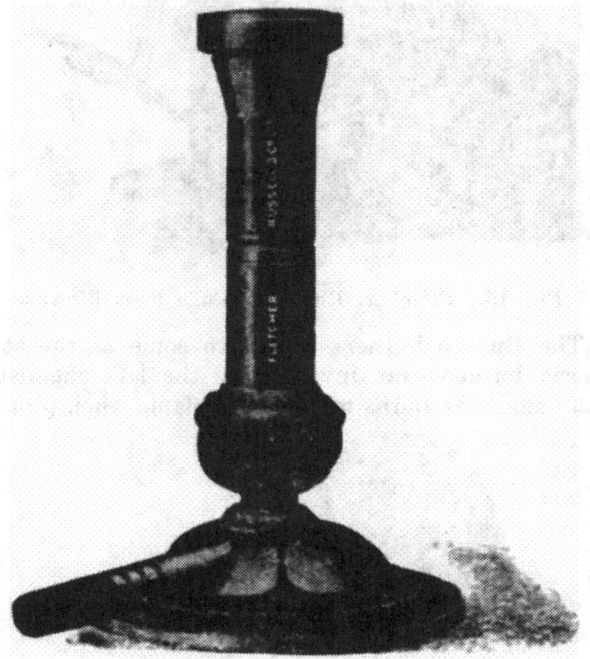

Fig. 17.—Fletcher, Russell & Co.'s Safety Bunsen.

To make a Bunsen burner the following materials will be necessary : A piece of brass tube 3½ in. long, ½ in. external diameter ; another, ⅜ in. in diameter, 1½ in. long ; a brass flange similar to those on an ordinary bracket, but without a tap ; a brass elbow ; also a piece of brass tubing about 1 in. long having a very fine bore.

Commence by soldering the elbow-piece on to the brass flange and make sure that the branch which has a screw cut upon it, is uppermost. If the large tube is not of very thick brass, it will be a little too large to fit this screwed part; if so, cut out a piece of thin sheet brass, ½ in. by 1¼ in., turn it up into a cylinder and solder *inside* the large tube; then tap the tube inside so that it will screw on the male thread of the elbow-piece. Near the end of the large tube which has been threaded drill two holes diameterwise, each about ⅜ in. diameter, exactly opposite to each other, and with their centre ⅜ in. from the end of the tube.

Fig. 18.—Fletcher, Russell & Co.'s Laboratory Bunsen.

The tube with fine bore is for the gas to pass through, and is required to be soldered inside the vertical tube of the elbow piece, and allowed to project about half an inch. If it is too small, fill around it with a little sheet lead; keep the small tube perfectly vertical and in the centre of the outer tube, then solder. When the larger outer tube has been screwed on, and the ⅜ in. tube screwed into the side elbow, the burner is theoretically complete. Fix the indiarubber tube from the gas supply on to the side tube, and test the burner. If the flame has a purplish-blue colour, the air and gas are being delivered to the burner in the right proportion. If the flame is yellow at the tip there is too much gas, so slightly close up the hole in the small tube. If the

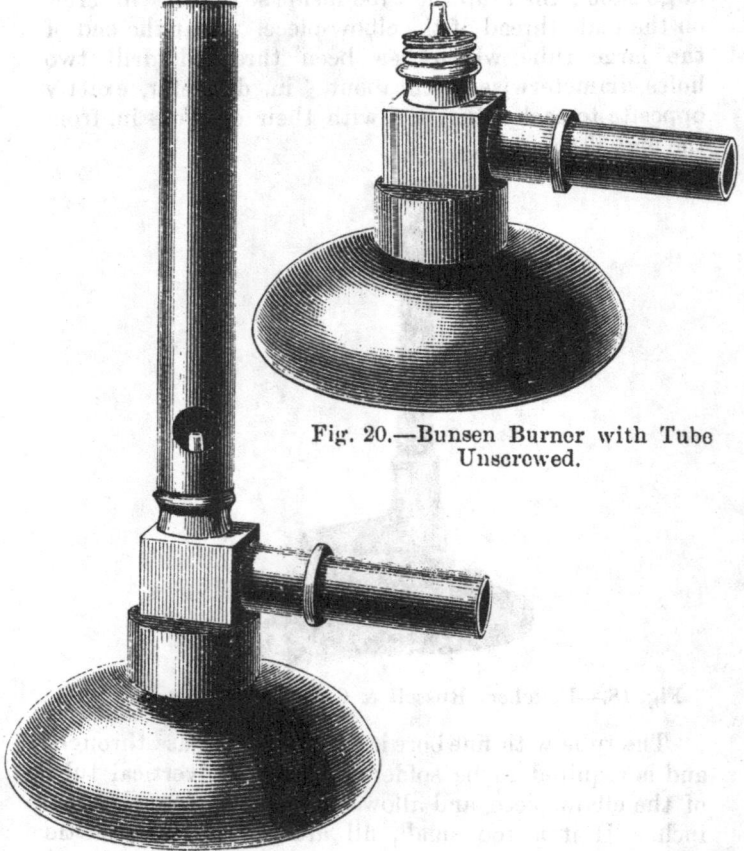

Fig. 20.—Bunsen Burner with Tube Unscrewed.

Fig. 19.—Home-made Bunsen Burner.

gas burns with a green flame and hissing noise, then the air supply is too large. To remedy this, cut out a piece of sheet brass about ¾ in. wide and 1¾ in. long, and drill in it two holes, each ⅜ in. in diameter, and at a distance apart to correspond with the holes drilled through the large tube; turn it up into the form of a tube, and push it over the large tube of burner until it covers the air-holes. By turning it to make the holes correspond more or less, the delivery of the air may be regulated.

If the Bunsen burner is needed for blowpipe work, the following arrangement will be found very useful for supporting the blowpipe, and will allow of the flame being blown downwards upon a charcoal or other support. Get a piece of brass tube 4 in. long, ⅜ in. in

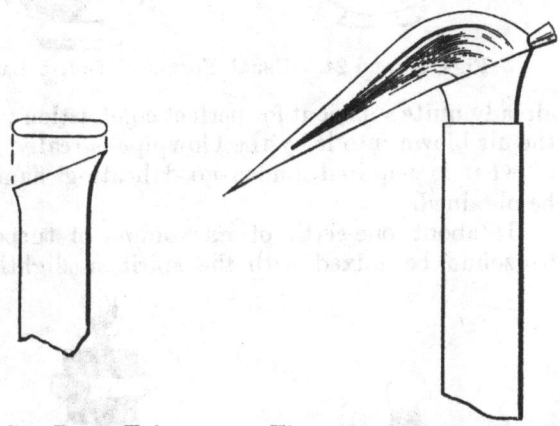

Fig. 21.—Cut Brass Tube for Bunsen Burner.   Fig. 22.—Directed Flame of Burner.

diameter. Cut obliquely at one end (Fig. 21); soften this end by heating in the flame of the burner, and quench it in water, and then flatten it out carefully until the opening is a mere narrow slit. By dropping this inside the tube of the burner, and closing the air-holes, a wide flame will result, which, by resting the nozzle of the blowpipe on the edge of the tube, may be blown downwards or upwards as required (Fig. 22).

In place of a Bunsen burner, the spirit lamp will do for all operations, though not so well. When a great heat is required, a flat spirit lamp, similar to those used with a camp-kettle, may be tried; or a layer of asbestos may be placed in the lid of a tin box, and this, soaked with spirit, will give a hot flame; both of these flames rapidly burn out, and the spirit needs replenishing often.

The spirit lamp is not suitable for experiments with the mouth blowpipe. The supply of air to the flame is

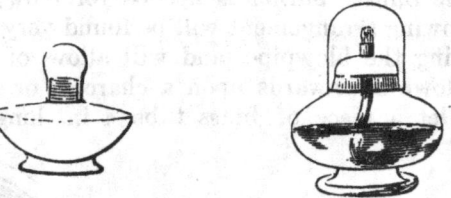

Figs. 23 and 24.—Usual Forms of Spirit Lamp.

already quite sufficient for perfect combustion; therefore the air blown into it by the blowpipe is really in excess of what is required, and a good heating flame cannot be obtained.

If about one-sixth of its volume of turpentine or benzoline be mixed with the spirit, a slightly smoky

Fig. 25.—Spirit Lamp with Stoppered Side Neck.

Fig. 26.—Home-made Spirit Lamp.

flame is obtained, which is much more suitable for blowpipe work. In conjunction with this, it may be found best also to flatten the wick-holder slightly at the top, so that a flat wick is obtained.

The spirit lamp usually employed consists of a glass vessel to hold the spirit, with an earthenware or brass tube in its mouth through which the wick passes; over this is a glass cap ground to fit on the lower vessel so as to prevent evaporation when the lamp is not in use (see Figs. 23, 24, and 25).

To make a cheap form of the glass spirit lamp, obtain a two-ounce wide-mouthed bottle and a cork to fit it, the metal portion of a penholder, some unwoven cotton wick, and methylated spirit. By means of pliers break off the portion of the pen-holder which grips the nib, and thus leave a short steel tube. Make a hole in the centre of the cork to receive the tube, which is pushed half-way through. Make a smaller hole in the cork by means of red-hot wire; this will allow air to enter as the spirit escapes. Pull the wick through the tube, as shown in Fig. 26. Put some spirit in the bottle, cork up the mouth, and the spirit lamp is ready for lighting.

CHAPTER II.

MANIPULATING GLASS TUBING.

THE materials used for glass-blowing are neither many nor expensive, all that are requisite being glass tubing in the diameters shown by Fig. 27, glass rod (Fig. 28), a sharp triangular file, a triangular tool of sheet copper mounted in a wooden handle (Fig. 29), pieces of charcoal sharpened to the shape shown in Fig. 30, and a small piece of beeswax.

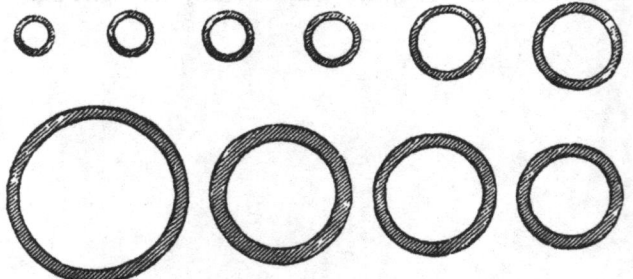

Fig. 27.—Sections of Glass Tubing.

There are several kinds of glass tubing made—soft soda glass, lead glass, and hard glass, the first-named being the best fitted for ordinary work. Good glass tubing should be free from bubbles, knots, and parallel lines; when scratched with a file and broken, it should leave a straight end; when brought into the flame it should not crack, nor become opaque, nor become covered with a fine powder.

In using the blowpipe if the gas be turned on only slightly, so that a small flame is given on blowing gently, a long, fine-pointed, very hot flame will be obtained; with this, only local heating of an object is possible (Fig. 31). This flame may be called the small flame. On admitting more gas and air, a large non-luminous flame results, which, though not so hot as the

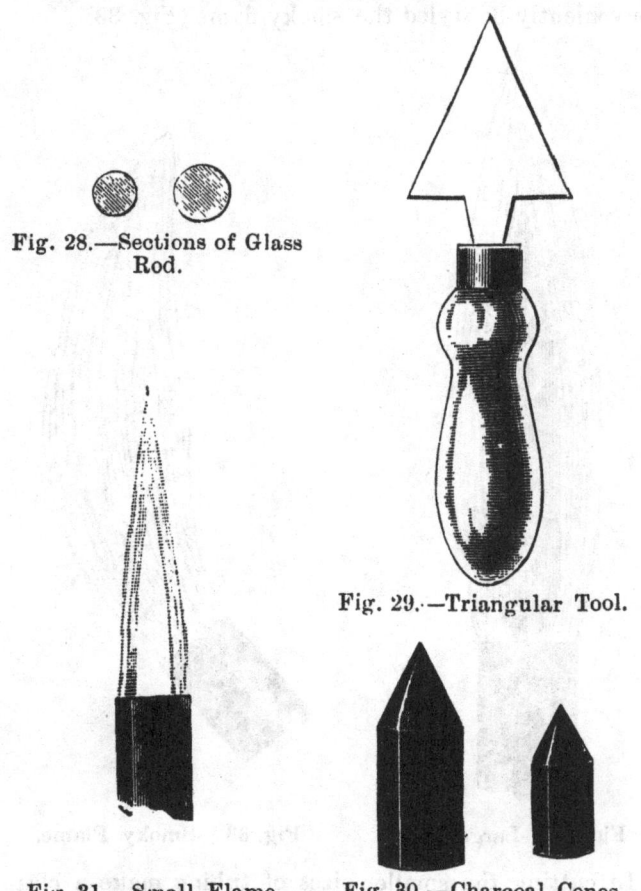

Fig. 28.—Sections of Glass Rod.

Fig. 29.—Triangular Tool.

Fig. 31.—Small Flame.   Fig. 30.—Charcoal Cones.

last, heats more gradually, and over a much greater area. This flame is the one most often used, and may be called the large flame (Fig. 32).

By ceasing to blow, a large, luminous, smoky flame is obtained, which is very useful for annealing hot glass; it cools objects gradually, and covers them with a non-conducting coating of carbon or soot, which protects them from currents of cold air. This flame may conveniently be styled the smoky flame (Fig. 33).

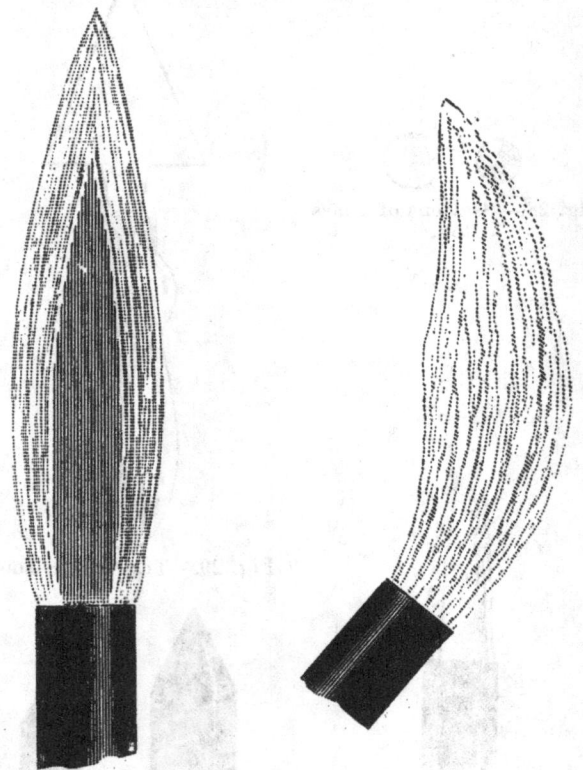

Fig. 32.—Large Flame.   Fig. 33.—Smoky Flame.

In cutting the smaller sizes of tubing make a clean file mark partly round the tube at the point to be severed, take the tube in both hands, place a thumb upon each side of the mark (Fig. 34), and bend slightly in a downward direction; the tube should sever cleanly. Large sizes, about $\frac{1}{2}$ in. up to $\frac{3}{4}$ in., may be cut by making a file mark as before, and bringing this part down on the edge of the bench sharply. For tubes over ¾ in., it is necessary to place a piece of red hot glass rod on the file mark. Treated once or twice in this way they generally sever; if not, a drop of water will produce a crack which may be carried around by judicious use of the hot rod.

In bending tubes with an ordinary gas jet, have a

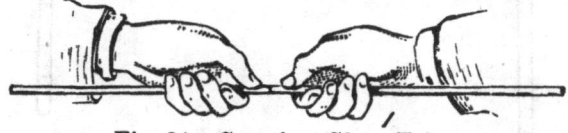

Fig. 34.—Severing Glass Tube.

flame about 1½ in. wide; hold the tube on each side of the flame at the tip of the bright portion (Fig. 35), turning it round all the time, so that it may be equally heated. When the glass commences to soften, apply a very gentle bending force in the direction to produce a curve like that at Fig. 36, and not as at Fig. 37, which is badly made, and very liable to crack. During the heating, the tube will have become coated with

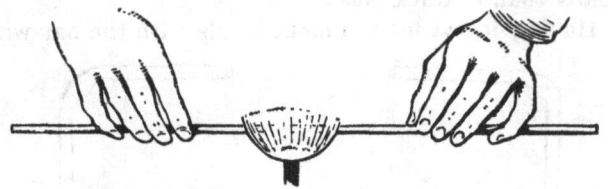

Fig. 35.—Method of Bending Glass Tube.

a deposit of soot. This is a bad conductor of heat, and, if not removed, will allow the glass to cool slowly. Place the tube resting against a block of wood, so that the bend may not come in contact with any cold surface. When cold, proceed to bend the other end slightly. The end which is being heated in the flame cannot be held, so when the glass is soft enough, give it a touch with a piece of charcoal to bring it to the required shape allow to cool again, wipe off the soot, and proceed to round off the rough ends of the tube. For this purpose, hold each end in the flame issuing from the Bunsen burner, and gradually bring it down into the hottest part of the flame. The ends will then fuse slightly, and be rendered stronger, neater, and much less liable to crack. Cool down each end by blackening

Fig. 36.—Neatly-bent Tube.   Fig. 37.—Badly-bent Tube.

it in the smoky flame produced by cutting off the air supply.

A great necessity in heating glass is to increase the heat very slowly, and to cool the object down very gradually; otherwise fracture is almost sure to ensue. In working thin glass such great precaution is not required, as the heat is conducted better and more equally than in thick glass.

Having learnt how to make bends with the batswing

Figs. 38 and 39.—Badly-bent Tubes.

flame, proceed to bend tubes with the blowpipe. Hold a tube in the large blowpipe flame so that the centre is heated, move the tube from side to side, and at the same time rotate gently so that a large part of it is equally heated. As soon as the glass commences to soften remove it from the flame, place a finger upon one end, gently blow at the other, and gradually bring the tube to a right angle. The blowing must be gentle and continuous during the whole time of the bending, to prevent the tube collapsing. Care should also be taken

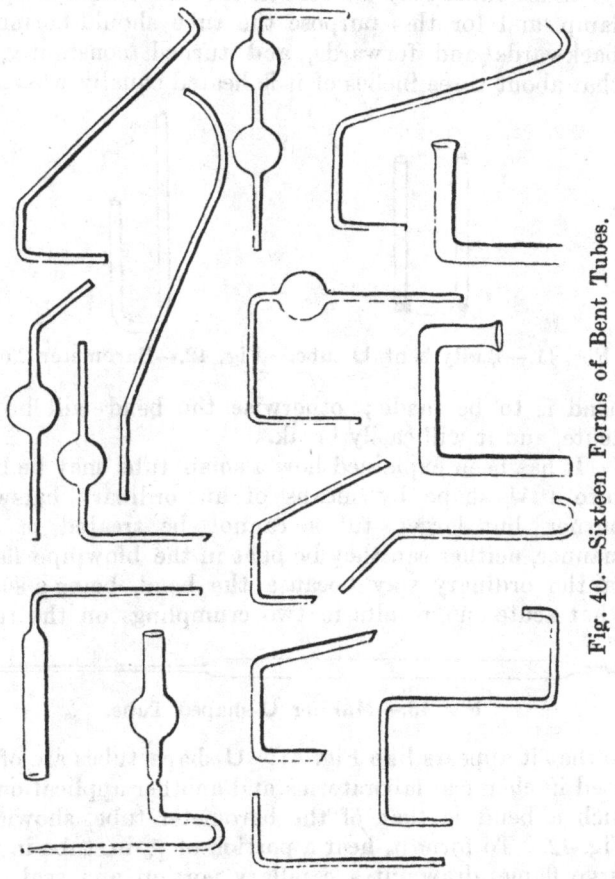

Fig. 40.—Sixteen Forms of Bent Tubes.

not to force the tube; if the glass is not soft enough replace it in the flame. The correct heat will be found by practice. A good bend is shown at Fig. 36, bad bends at Figs. 37, 38, and 39; the first bad one is due to heat being too local or to bending too quickly, the second to insufficient blowing, and the third to excessive blowing, or excessive heat. Sixteen other forms of bends are shown in Fig. 40.

Glass tubes may be bent in the flame of the spirit-lamp, and for this purpose the tube should be moved backwards and forwards, and turned constantly, so that about three inches of it is heated equally where the

Fig. 41.—Badly bent U-tube.   Fig. 42.—Barometer Tube.

bend is to be made; otherwise the bend will be too acute, and it will easily break.

It has been explained how a small tube may be bent into a U shape by means of an ordinary batswing burner, but larger tubes cannot be treated in this manner, neither can they be bent in the blowpipe flame in the ordinary way because the bend, being a somewhat acute one, results in two crumplings on the tube,

Fig. 43.—Making U-shaped Tube.

so that it appears like Fig. 41. U-shape tubes are often used in chemical laboratories, and another application of such a bend is that of the barometer tube, shown at Fig. 42. To form it, heat a portion of $\frac{5}{18}$-in. tube in the large flame, draw out a capillary portion, and seal off; about six inches further on the tube again heat it, draw out and seal off; the tube will then appear like Fig. 43. Break the capillary end, A, and rotate the tube in the large flame, so that as much as possible of the centre of the tube may be heated, supporting the

Manipulating Glass Tubing.

tube well, otherwise the centre will fall downwards and become unmanageable. Having brought the centre of the tube to a uniform red heat, withdraw it from the flame, and blow in at the open end. The tube will swell out to the shape shown in Fig. 44; at the same time draw out the tube, and bend it into the form of a U (Fig. 45).

Fig. 44.—Making U-shaped Tube.

Here three processes have to be carried on simultaneously—the blowing, drawing, and bending. They must be done quickly, or the glass will cool down before the final shape is acquired; blowing thins the walls of the tube, and the larger portion thus produced must be drawn down again to the size of the tube. In this way new tube is produced which goes to form the bend;

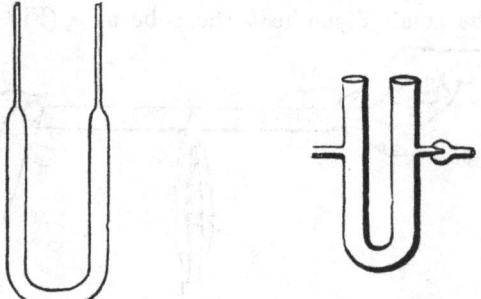

Fig. 45.—U-shaped Tube.   Fig. 46.—U-tube.

the bent portion is, therefore, thinner than the remainder of the tube.

A point to be emphasised is, never work with the glass hotter than is absolutely necessary—for instance, in bending small tubes the temperature should be much lower than that for blowing bulbs. Other and more difficult forms of U-tubes are illustrated by Figs. 46, 47, and 48.

The method of sealing glass tubes varies with their size and the purpose for which the tubes are required. In making test tubes and small tubes for holding specimens, proceed as follows :— Hold a piece of ½-inch tube 10 in. long in the large blowpipe flame so that the

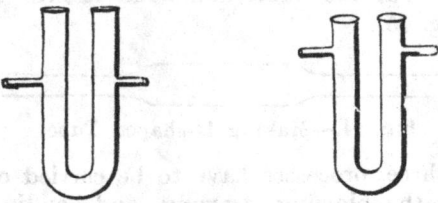

Figs. 47 and 48.—U-tubes.

centre only is heated, and gently rotate (Fig. 49). When the glass has become thoroughly pasty, remove from the flame, and withdraw the hands from each other with a slight twisting motion (Fig. 50). Endeavour to keep the capillary tube as near as possible concentric. Now with the small flame heat the tube at A (Fig. 51), and,

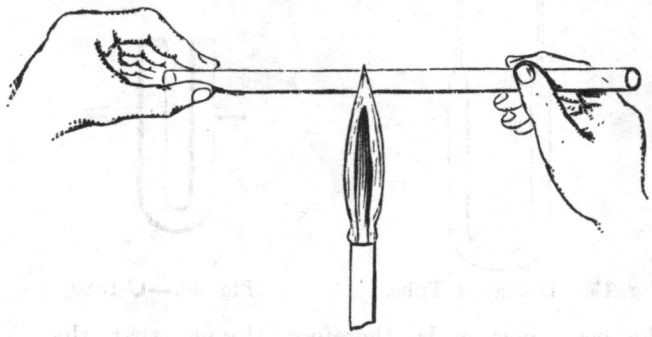

Fig. 49.—Heating Tube.

when melted, draw away the capillary portion. Lay aside the half of the tube, having the fine part attached, and proceed with the other portion. Heat it in the large flame until the end becomes somewhat rounded with a small knob of glass adhering, and at once proceed to remove this projection. Lower the flame, and play upon the knob only (Fig. 52). Bring a glass rod against it, and draw away some of the glass. Continue doing so until the knob has disappeared or almost so. Turn up

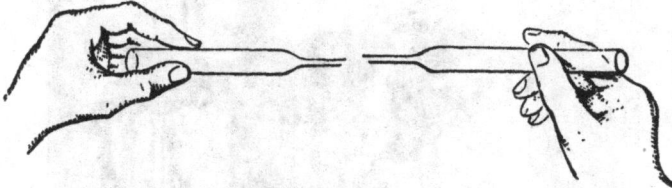

Fig. 50.—Drawing Tube.

the flame again, heat the whole end of the tube, remove from the flame, place the open end in the mouth, and blow gently, at the same time rotating the tube, so as to

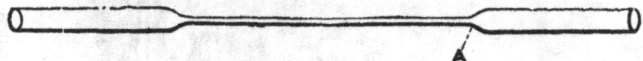

Fig. 51.—Drawing Tube.

obtain a neat, rounded end. The second portion of the tube may then be treated in the same manner.

It is not necessary to take precautions against

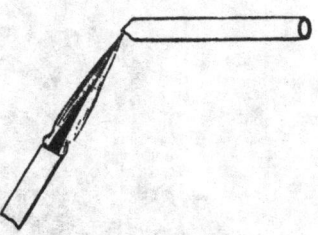

Fig. 52.—Sealing Tube.

cracking when working with good glass, but in ordinary work, hold the end in the smoky flame until covered with soot, and then rest it against a block of wood. Hot glass should on no account be placed upon a cold surface. The method of drawing glass tubes on a large scale is illustrated in Fig. 53.

36   GLASS WORKING.

Fig. 53.—Drawing Glass Tubes on Large Scale.

In order to blow out a neat bottom to the tube or other articles which will be referred to, it is necessary to hold the tube horizontal, or nearly so. The end of the tube should be placed loosely in the mouth, not touched with the teeth and not gripped in any way by the lips. The lips should only touch it sufficiently to make an air-tight seal. The blowing should be very steady, slight at first while the glass is hot, but gradu-

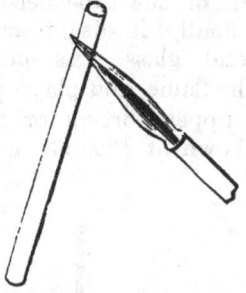

Fig. 54.—Slanting Tube in Flame.

ally increasing as the glass cools. If the blowing be too strong at first, the bottom of the tube will swell out into a bubble and burst. During the blowing, the tube should be rotated slowly backward and forward, the fingers, of course, never leaving the tube. The backward

Fig. 55.—Properly-sealed Tube. Fig. 56.—Badly-sealed Tube.

and forward rotation of the tube must be carried on during the whole time of heating and blowing; counting one, two, will facilitate this.

Sometimes it is necessary to seal up a substance inside of a tube which has to withstand high pressure from within. In order to do this satisfactorily, first seal up one end of the tube in the manner just described, allowing a moderately thick bottom. Place the substance in the tube, then hold it in a slanting direction in the large flame (Fig. 54), rotate the tube, and gently draw out a portion of it. Heat the tube slightly, and rotate, but do not draw out the tube further. Allow the glass to fall gradually inwards, so that the bore of the tube becomes narrower and narrower, until finally it disappears entirely, leaving a thread of solid glass. As soon as this object is attained, lower the flame, and play upon the solid part. Draw away the upper portion of the tube. A well-sealed tube is shown at Fig. 55, a badly-sealed tube at Fig. 56.

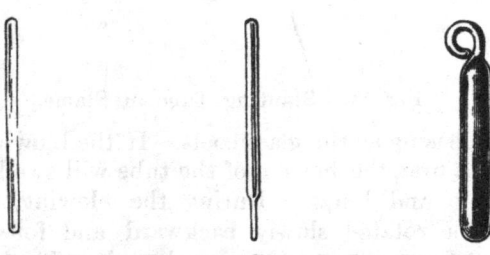

Fig. 57.—Glass Rod Stirrer. Fig. 58.—Glass Rod for Dropping Purposes. Fig. 59.—Barometer Float.

In working glass rod, it must be heated more carefully than glass tube, otherwise it flies to pieces, because it is thicker. Always hold it for a few seconds in the hot air from the blowpipe, and gradually bring it into the flame. The thicker the glass rod, the more carefully must this preliminary heating be carried out.

For practice make a few stirrers. Cut off several lengths of the rod, the most convenient sizes being 4 in., 6 in., and 8 in. Hold each end of these in the hot air of the blowpipe, and bring gradually into the flame; in a very short time the ends will become rounded (Fig. 57). They may then be laid down with the hot ends resting against a block of wood or off the edge of the bench.

Annealing will not be necessary unless the rods are thick.

For rods for dropping purposes, heat a piece of glass rod 8 in. long in the centre, and as soon as the glass becomes pasty withdraw from the flame; pull the hands apart slowly, at the same time imparting a twisting motion to the rod. Draw the centre portion down until it is about the thickness of a knitting needle, and get it as straight as possible. Now cut through the central part, leaving about an inch of the tapered portion on each tube. Round off the pointed ends in the small flame (Fig. 58).

Sometimes a rod like Fig. 59 is required—for instance, as a barometer float. Draw out a portion of rod, as in the last example, sever it at the centre, then hold the smaller part of the rod in the flame. Only warm it gently, and press a piece of charcoal against it carefully until it bends round into a hook shape. As soon as it touches the thicker part of the rod, increase the heat at the junction until the glass fuses up, forming an unbroken ring.

A hot glass rod is useful for severing tubes. For this purpose it should be drawn to a point in a similar way to those for dropping rods, the fine portion alone being heated and then placed upon the file mark.

Some persons prefer to use a charcoal point, which, when once lighted, continues to glow, whilst others use string dipped in turpentine, etc.; but the effectiveness of the glass rod can be depended upon. By means of it, retorts, flasks, beakers, glass shades, bottles, gas globes, etc., may be cut up, and utilised in one way or another, as will be described later.

Those who intend learning how to manufacture fancy goods will have to practise drawing out soft glass rod, as the fine thread-like portions of the model ships, small glass rings, etc., on ornaments, are made in this manner.

To finish the mouth of a test-tube, hold the tube in the

full flame of the blowpipe in a slanting position, so that the mouth only is heated. Allow the glass to fall in slightly, then remove from the flame. Place a charcoal cone in the mouth of the tube, and give one or two turns so as to force out the mouth to a slight extent. This will give a finish to the tube, and, at the same time, add strength to the open end (Fig. 60). The opening out of tubes in this manner can be more neatly carried out with

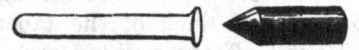

Fig. 60.—Finishing Mouth of Tube.

the triangular tool (Fig. 29), but it is better to practise first with the charcoal cones. Tubes under ½ in. diameter may be treated in the same way, using, however, a piece of stiff iron wire instead of the cone. The iron wire must be held at a slight angle with the mouth of the tube, and the latter rotated against it (Fig. 61).

To join together two tubes, take a portion of tube $\frac{3}{16}$ in. in diameter and cut a piece having at least one end perfectly true. Take another portion of the same tube

Fig. 61.—Finishing Mouth of Tube.

about 5 in. long and with both ends cut true. Hold this second portion in the large flame so that the central part is heated, then quickly draw out to a capillary tube; hold the finer portion in the flame for a second and then draw the hands away, thus severing it, forming two tubes like Fig. 62. Now take up the first portion of the tube in the right hand and one of the second pieces in the left hand; hold each of them in the edge of the large flame (Fig. 63) so that their mouths alone are heated, rotate, and, before the glass falls in too much, bring them gently together while in the flame. This results in the tubes being cemented one to the other, the join, however, being thick and readily seen ; and it is most probable that if the tube was allowed to cool down in this condition the joint would be the weakest part of it. Care must be taken in pressing the tubes together,

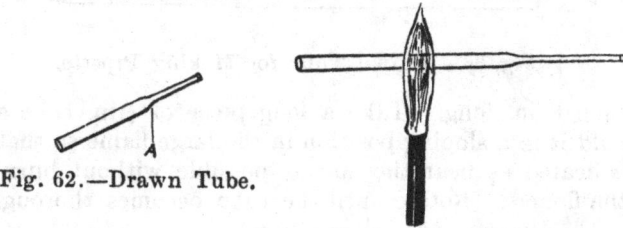

Fig. 62.—Drawn Tube.

Fig. 63.—Joining Tubes in Flame.

because a touch only is required, and more than this results in the joint being unduly thickened, or what is worse, the junction is pressed out of shape and cannot possibly be put right again. Fig. 64 shows the appearance of the tube at this stage.

Fig. 64.—Roughly-jointed Tube.

Continue to heat the thickened part of the tube, supporting the fine tube with the left hand, as shown in previous exercises, and rotating with the right hand ; then withdraw and blow a very tiny bulb right on the junction (Fig. 65) ; in this way the thickening is got rid

Fig. 65.—Jointed Tube containing Bulb.

of and the joint secured. Heat the bulb very slightly, remove again from the flame, then with a twisting motion draw the hands away from each other until the bulb disappears, being drawn until it is of the same diameter as the tube. The joint, if properly made will scarcely be distinguishable.

It is often necessary to joint a large to a small diameter tube in making bulb pipettes, etc.; in such a case tubes often as much as 1 in. in diameter are fused to others not more than $\frac{3}{16}$ in.

As an exercise, cut off two portions of $\frac{3}{16}$-in. tube,

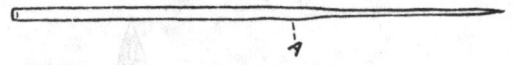

Fig. 66.—Drawn Tube for Making Pipette.

each 8 in. long. Take a long piece of $\frac{1}{2}$-in. tube and hold it in a sloping position in the large flame so that it is heated as near the end as possible without burning the fingers. Rotate until the tube becomes thoroughly

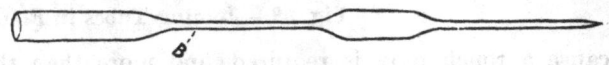

Fig. 67.—Tube for making Pipette.

heated, then withdraw it from the flame and remove the upper portion with a gentle rotating motion. Seal off the tube, and thus leave the end like Fig. 66. Again heat the tube at a point about 2 in. lower, remove, and

Fig. 68.—Tube for making Pipette.

draw out a second portion (Fig. 67). Seal off at B, and the tube will then appear like Fig. 68. Break one of the fine points, B. Hold the bulb tube in the small flame so that the point A may be heated; the fine tube

Fig. 69.—Tube for making Pipette.

quickly fuses, and may then be withdrawn (Fig. 69). Continue heating the end, using a larger flame, then remove, and, by blowing in at the fine tube, the closed portion is made to assume a rounded form (Fig. 70). Now lower the flame again, and play upon the tip of this rounded part. When thoroughly red hot, remove and blow vigorously so as to burst the end ; remove the loose glass, when the tube will present the appearance

Fig. 70.—Tube for making Pipette.

shown at Fig. 71. The end of the fine tube should now be sealed up by holding it in the flame for a few seconds.

A smaller tube may now be sealed on. Remove the

Fig. 71.—Tube for making Pipette.

bulb tube to the left hand, and take up one of the $\frac{3}{16}$-in. tubes in the right hand; bring the two into opposite sides of the flame in a horizontal position (Fig. 72). As soon as they have attained a welding temperature, bring

Fig. 72.—Making Pipette.

them gently together so as to form one tube ; of course there will be a thickened ring at the point shown at A (Fig. 73), to remove which place the junction in the small flame, rotate, and blow out a small bulb so as to

Fig. 73.—Making Pipette.

get rid of the thickening at this part (Fig. 74); then heat the bulb slightly, and, by drawing and twisting, reduce this to the diameter of the smaller tube. Fig. 75 shows what is meant.

The tube has now been sealed on. Before proceeding further it will be best to break the capillary end again and then seal up the end of the tube which has just been joined. Instead of sealing this tube it may be found more convenient to cut by means of a cork-borer a small cork that will fit it air-tight, and place this in

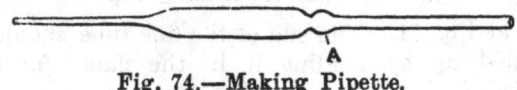

Fig. 74.—Making Pipette.

the open end of the tube to prevent the escape of air when sealing on a second tube. The sealing of the second tube is carried out exactly as with the first one. One of the tubes should be drawn out and the end rounded for a bulb pipette (Fig. 76).

To make three- and four-way tubes take a portion of

Fig. 75.—Making Pipette.

the ¼-in. tube about 8 in. long, also a portion of the $\frac{3}{16}$-in. tube about 6 in. long. Hold the latter in the flame, draw out and seal off in the same manner as was described when joining tubes of equal diameter, and then allow both pieces to cool. Hold the wider piece of tube in the flame until it seals up at one end entirely,

Fig 76.—Bulb Pipette.

then remove and blow a small bulb. Hold the larger tube in the small flame so that only a very small portion at A (Fig. 77) is heated; remove and blow hard so as to raise a small knob or bulb at that part of the tube (Fig. 78). Still using a small flame, play upon the end of the knob, rotating the tube as usual, and as soon as it becomes thoroughly red hot remove and blow very violently so that the bulb may be burst. Carefully remove all the fine glass before proceeding further, and the tube will then appear like Fig. 79. Move the larger tube into the left hand, take up one of the smaller tubes with the

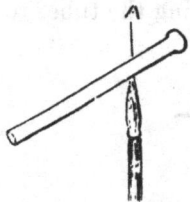

Fig. 77.—Joining and Jointing Tubes.

right, and hold them together in a moderately large flame; the opening of the larger tube should be somewhat inclined towards the worker, and should be the

Fig. 78.   Fig. 79.
Figs. 78 and 79.—Joining and Jointing Tubes.

only part heated (Fig. 80). The heating will take only a very short time; care should be taken not to carry it so far that too much of the glass melts. As soon as the

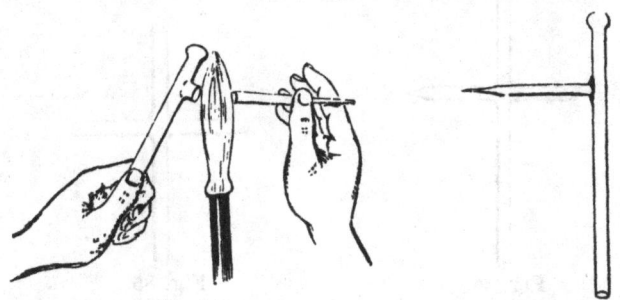

Fig. 80.   Fig. 81.
Figs. 80 and 81.—Joining and Jointing Tubes.

glass is red hot, bring the two openings gently together, and at the same time blow gently at the open end of the larger tube to prevent the glass falling in. The object aimed at in this is to bring the smaller tube perfectly straight upon the other, so that the joint may be sealed all round at the first touch (Fig. 81). If successful in this, of course there will be no escape of air on blowing. The method of bringing the tubes together must also be

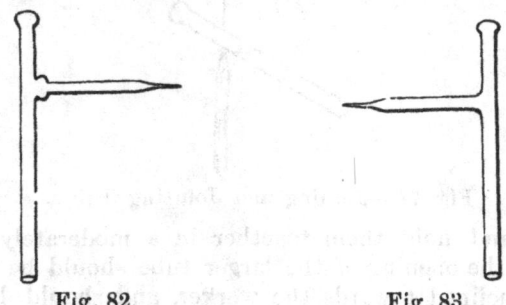

Fig. 82. Fig. 83.
Figs. 82 and 83.—Joining and Jointing Tubes.

studied, in order that a light touch may be gained, otherwise crooked or thickened joints will result.

Turn down the flame a little, hold the tube in it so that the joint is heated, rotate the tube carefully so that no pressure is thrown on the joint, then remove and

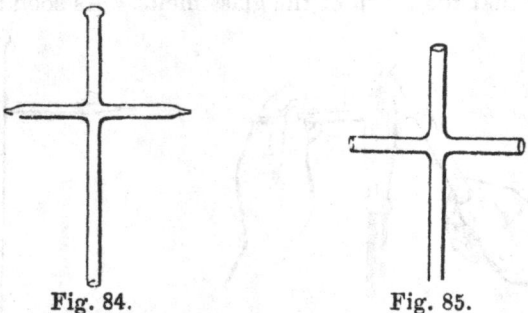

Fig. 84. Fig. 85.
Figs. 84 and 85 —Joining and Jointing Tubes.

blow gently until a small bulb is produced (Fig. 82). If in the first instance the joint was not entirely an airtight one, it may be made so by several judicious heatings and blowings until the escape of air is stopped; when the joint is airtight, blow a small bulb. Heat this

Manipulating Glass Tubing. 47

small bulb slightly, still rotating the tube; remove, and by a gentle twisting and pulling motion combined, draw the bulb to the size of the smaller tube; keep up a slight blowing during this process, because the glass is so thin that it may give way and spoil the joint, which should appear like Fig. 83 when finished.

This piece, after the closed ends have been cut off, is,

Fig. 86.—Glass Blowing on Large Scale.

of course, a three-way tube. From this a four-way tube may be made by heating it at any point most convenient, and sealing on a second tube in a manner similar to the

48   GLASS WORKING.

first (Fig. 84); the closed ends are then cut off, thus obtaining a four-way tube (Fig. 85).

Some idea of the scene in a glass foundry where glass blowing on a large scale is being carried on may be gleaned from Fig. 86, in which may be seen two operators standing near the furnaces. The tube in the hands and at the lips of one of the men is of iron, and has hanging from it a pasty mass of glass to be blown or moulded into a flask or similar article.

CHAPTER III.

BLOWING BULBS AND FLASKS.

To blow small bulbs, hold one end of a piece of tubing about 8 in. long and $\frac{3}{16}$ in. diameter in the large blowpipe flame, the tube sloping upwards so that the end is highly heated. The tube soon closes up, and a lump of pasty glass collects upon the closed end. As soon as this is the case, withdraw the tube from the flame, hold it in a horizontal position, blow into the open end, rotating it all the time and observing the precaution not to stop the tube at all, until a small spherical bulb about ½ in. diameter is obtained. Practise this exercise a few times, varying the size of the bulb from ¼ in. to ½ in. The smaller sized bulb tubes may be cut down to 4 in., and will then be found useful for heating substances in qualitative analysis. Some examples of small bulb tubes are given in Figs. 87, 88, 89, 90, 91, and 92.

To make a small flask, choose a portion of the $\frac{3}{16}$-in. tube 8 in. long, hold it in a slanting position (Fig. 93) in the large blowpipe flame, and as soon as the end has closed, and the lump of pasty glass collected, withdraw from the flame, and blow a small bulb about ½ in. diameter upon the end (Fig. 91). Hold the tube again in the flame, this time in a horizontal position (Fig. 94), and heat it at a point just beyond the bulb first blown; rotate the tube between the thumb and first three fingers of the right hand. When the heated part of the tube is sufficiently softened, again withdraw, and blow a second small bulb similar to and alongside the first one (Fig. 95).

Replace the tube in the flame and heat both the bulbs at the same time; they will gradually fall together into one elongated or pear-shaped bulb (Fig. 96). Proceed to get this bulb at a bright red heat, and rotate rather quicker, or it will fall unequally to one side. Remove from the flame, place the tube in the mouth, and blow very gently; rotate the tube backward and forward as the bulb falls, so as to keep it exactly on the

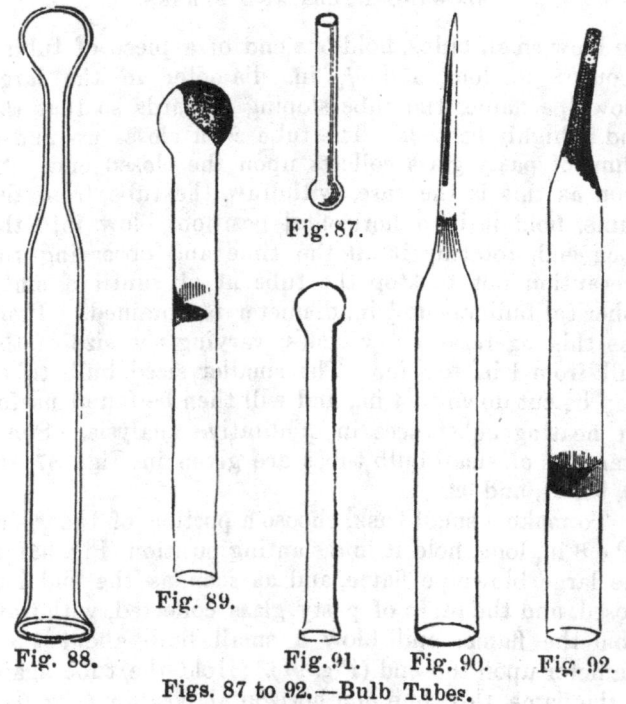

Figs. 87 to 92.—Bulb Tubes.

centre of the tube; gradually increase the blowing as the glass cools, until finally a perfectly spherical bulb about 1½ in. results (Fig. 97). This will probably require a little practice, but students generally blow very fair bulbs after the first two or three tries.

The bulb to be not too thin for ordinary purposes should be able to withstand a blow from the finger knuckle. In order to obtain this strength, it is

BLOWING BULBS AND FLASKS.

necessary that a fair amount of melted glass should be produced upon the tube, and that is the reason for blowing two bulbs and fusing them into one; a bulb might have been blown from the first one, but it would

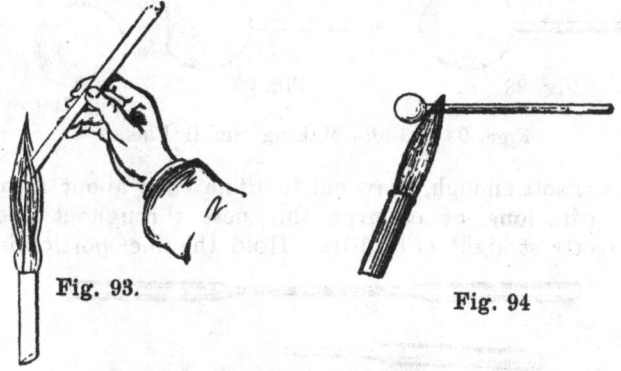

Figs. 93 and 94.—Making Small Flask.

have been too thin to be useful. Now turn down the flame to about half the usual height, and hold the bulb in the outer edge of it so that only the extreme

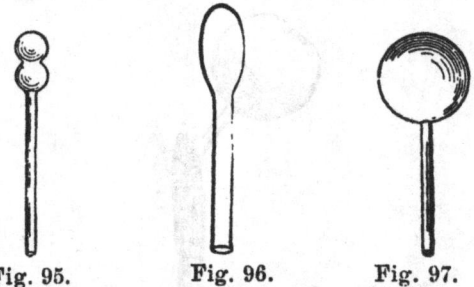

Figs. 95 to 97.—Making Small Flask.

bottom is heated. The tube should be held horizontal, and rotated steadily and rather quickly. The bottom will then fall in perfectly flat. Remove from the flame and blow it out slightly (Fig. 98); then as quickly suck inwards. The bottom will then appear as at Fig. 99. The flask may then be severed from the tube (Fig. 100).

To make larger flasks than these, hold a piece of ½-in. tube, 12 in. long, in the large flame, rotate, and, as soon

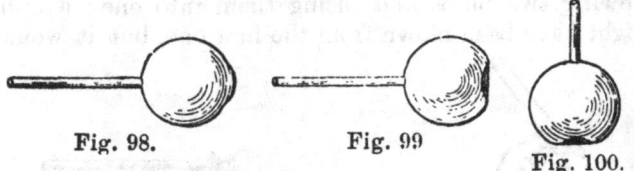

Fig. 98.   Fig. 99   Fig. 100.

Figs. 93 to 100.—Making Small Flask.

as it is soft enough, draw out to a fine tube about 8 in. or 10 in. long, of an even thickness throughout and perfectly straight (Fig. 101). Hold the finer portion in

Figs. 101 and 102.—Making Large Flask.

the flame and draw the two ends away, thus forming two similar tubes (Fig. 102). When these have cooled, take up one of them, break the pointed end, hold it in the

Fig. 103.—Making Large Flask.

large flame in the position shown at Fig. 93, rotate it, and, as soon as the end has closed up and sufficient glass collected, blow a small bulb upon it, hold the tube in a horizontal position, and bring it again into the flame at the point shown in Fig. 94. Rotate until hot enough, again remove, and blow a second bulb similar to the first; replace the tube a third time in the flame, heat it a little beyond the second bulb, remove, and blow still another bulb.

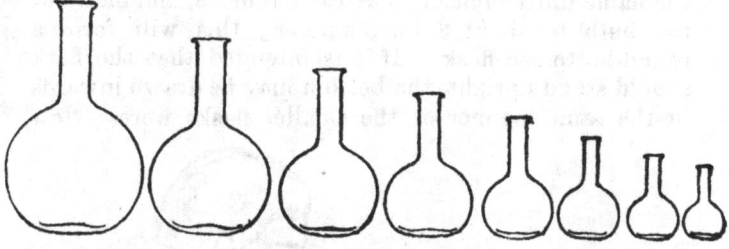

Fig. 104.—Set of Flasks.

Now proceed to fuse the three bulbs into one; and in order to do this satisfactorily some amount of practice and patience will be required. Heat the tube so that the first two bulbs become red hot; they will gradually lose their shape and fall into one elongated bulb; rotate the tube carefully so that the tendency of the hot glass

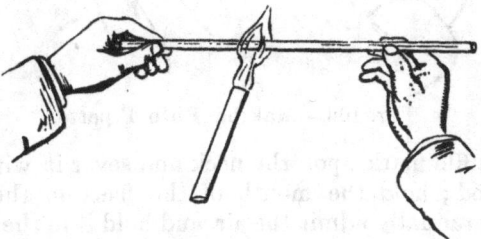

Fig. 105.—Making Bulb Pipette.

to fall may be obviated. As soon as the glass is soft enough, remove from the flame and carefully blow the bulb into a sphere of a diameter of not more than 1 in. Having now only two bulbs upon the tube, melt the small one into the large one in the same manner. There being more glass upon the end of the tube the tendency to fall will now be greater, and the glass must therefore be very carefully rotated to prevent this. Remove the tube from the flame and again blow the bulb; this time try to get it as nearly spherical as possible, and upon the centre of the tube. Place the bulb again in the flame until sufficiently red hot, remove, and blow out the bulb to about 3 in. diameter; this will form a round-bottomed flask. If it is intended that the flask should stand upright, the bottom may be drawn inwards in the same manner as the smaller flasks were. Now

Fig. 106.—Making Bulb Pipette.

make a file mark upon the neck and sever it with a hot glass rod; hold the mouth of the flask in the smoky flame, gradually admit the air, and hold it in the position shown at Fig. 103. As soon as the edge of the glass becomes red hot, remove from the flame and press out with a charcoal cone, forming a mouth to the flask. A set of flasks is shown in Fig. 104.

Before proceeding further, it will be necessary to give a few hints upon drawing, or decreasing the diameter of, a glass tube. To obtain small-sized tube, commence with the glass very hot, and draw rather quickly; if larger tube is required, the glass must not be so hot, and the drawing should be slower, thus regulating the size of the tube. The following examples will show how this is done.

To form plain pipettes, rotate a piece of the $\frac{3}{16}$-in. tube, 12 in. long, in the large flame till sufficiently heated, withdraw, hold it horizontally, and draw the hands apart from each other slowly with a slight twisting motion, so that the tube appears as in Fig. 101. Sever it in the centre, hold both ends of each tube in the flame to round them off, and two plain pipettes will result (Fig. 102).

If bulb pipettes are required, heat a piece of tube $\frac{1}{4}$ in. diameter and about 12 in. long, in the centre, and when sufficiently softened, remove and draw out quickly, producing a long, fine tube. Hold the fine tube a second in the flame and draw in two, sealing off each tube. Take up one of the pieces just produced, and

Fig. 107.—Making Bulb Pipette.

rotate it in the large flame in the position shown at Fig. 105. The left hand is in this case merely a support for the finer part of the tube; the latter must not be held in any way; the right hand is used for holding and rotating the tube. As soon as the tube is at a working temperature, remove it and hold it in the position shown at Fig. 106; slowly rotate with the right hand, still using the left hand only as a rest, and blow a small bulb upon the tube of about $\frac{1}{2}$ in. diameter.

Replace the tube in the flame, holding it in the same position as before, and heat it at a point slightly higher than the bulb just blown; remove again, and blow a second bulb (Fig. 107). Replace the tube in the flame; this time heat up both bulbs until they fuse into one, remove, and blow another small bulb. Finally, heat the bulbs, and blow out into one having a diameter of about 1½ in. If the pointed end of this be broken, it will then be a bulb pipette. The difficult part in the above operation is blowing the large bulb; it will be found that much practice will be required before a bulb can be obtained which is spherical, and which at the same time is directly upon the centre of the tube.

Fig. 108.—Badly made Bulb.

By holding the tube upon the forefingers and spinning it round, any unevenness will readily be detected; a carefully made bulb will spin round steadily and truly, but a badly made bulb will wobble in some directions.

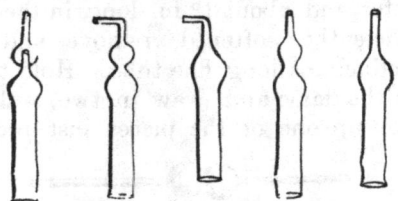

Fig. 109.—Bulb Tubes.

Fig. 108 shows the general tendency of a badly made bulb.

The bulb pipettes which are so often seen in chemical laboratories are made upon a plan different

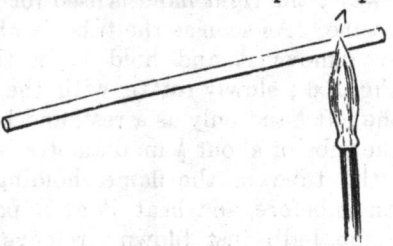

Fig. 110.—Making Bulb on Centre of Tube.

from those just described. The bulb is an elongated cylinder instead of a sphere. These pipettes are made from a wide piece of tube, which is jointed on to narrower pieces. Other forms of tubes with round bulbs are illustrated by Fig. 109.

To produce a bulb on the centre of a tube, hold a long piece of the ½-in. tube in a slanting position, so that one end rests against the bench; grasp the tube with both hands and rotate it, then with the large flame play

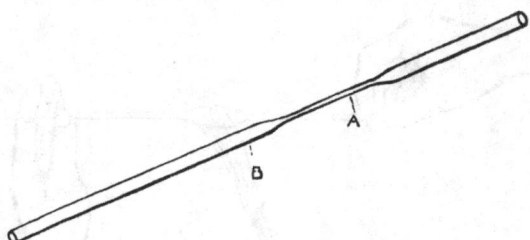

Fig. 111.—Making Bulb on Centre of Tube.

upon the point A (Fig. 110). When this part becomes thoroughly heated, withdraw the tube from the flame, and still inclining it, proceed to draw away the upper part, leaving a long capillary tube, A (Fig. 111). Seal this off by holding for a second in the flame. Next

Fig. 112.—Making Bulb on Centre of Tube.

allow the blowpipe to play upon the part B (Fig. 111), and when again sufficiently heated draw away a second time, producing another capillary portion, B, upon the tube (Fig. 112). Seal this off, leaving a tube like Fig. 113.

Care should be taken to get these tubes concentric

Fig. 113.—Making Bulb on Centre of Tube.

with the larger one, otherwise it will not be so easy to blow a well-shaped bulb afterwards.

Break one of the points off this tube, and hold it in a horizontal position so that the bulb A (Fig. 114) is alone heated. The flame should not be too high, or the softening of the fine tubes will allow the bulb to fall more than can be compensated for by rotating. Rotate the tube with the right hand, supporting it with the left hand as before described, and as soon as a bright red heat is attained, remove and blow a small bulb

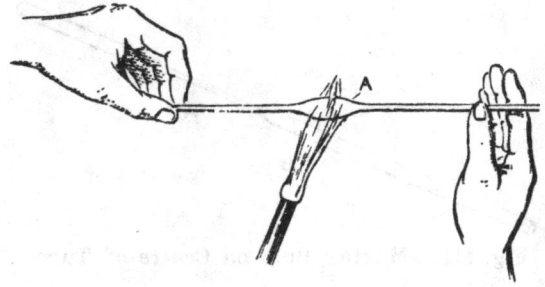

Fig. 114.—Making Bulb on Centre of Tube.

of about ¾ in. diameter; re-heat this bulb to the same temperature as before, again remove, and blow a bulb of about 1½ in. diameter. The first bulb may be blown with the tube inclined so that it may be watched, but

Fig. 115.—Bulb in Right Position.

the larger one will be better blown in a horizontal position. In order to produce a stout bulb, not too large but perfectly spherical and well balanced on the centre of the tube, some experience will be required, and

Fig. 116.—Making Bulb on Centre of Tube.

the rules already given must be adhered to. The tube must be supported, not held, by the left hand, but some little pressure upon the tube may be exercised with one of the fingers towards the end of the operation if the bulb is not quite straight, and this will tend to bring it into the proper position (Fig. 115). The bulbs generally made by beginners resemble Figs. 108 and 116 ; it will be seen that the latter, owing to the irregular rotation, is blown out too much at the one side.

To blow several bulbs upon one tube, heat a portion of the ½-in. tube in the large flame, draw away the upper portion and seal off the capillary tube ; heat the tube

Fig 117.—Blowing Several Bulbs on One Tube.

again about 4 in. lower down, and again draw out and seal off, producing a tube like Fig. 76, p. 44. Break the capillary end. Now turn the flame rather low, and hold the tube in it so that it may be locally heated at the position B; rotate slowly without drawing out at all, and the pasty glass will gradually fall in until it

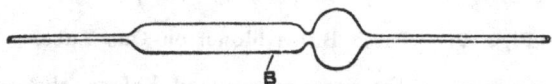

Fig. 118.—Blowing Several Bulbs on One Tube.

assumes the shape shown at Fig. 117. Withdraw from the flame and allow to remain until set, then turn up the flame and heat the bulb, A ; rotate the tube slowly, using the finger and thumb of the left hand as a rest, and then withdraw from the flame, and blow out the bulb to about twice its original size (Fig. 118).

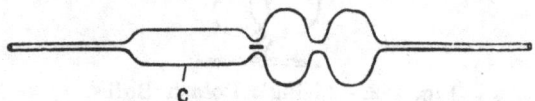

Fig. 119.—Blowing Several Bulbs on One Tube.

Again turn down the flame, and heat the tube at the point B ; allow the glass to fall in again as before, then remove. Now heat the bulb, and blow out to as near as possible the same size as the last one (Fig. 119). Lastly, heat the tube at C, and blow this out to the size of the others, thus forming a three-bulb tube (Fig. 120).

These bulbs may be more or less flattened by holding the capillary tube with the finger and thumb of the left hand, and pressing upwards when each bulb is assuming its proper size. This method of treatment is opposite to that used in producing oval bulbs as described on p. 61.

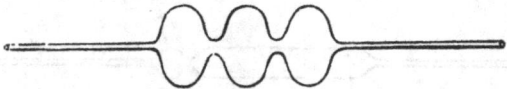

Fig. 120.—Three Bulbs blown on One Tube.

Fig. 121 shows a set of three bulbs joined together by longer tubes than the last. The method of making such a set of bulbs is very similar to that just described, but after each connecting portion has been produced, it

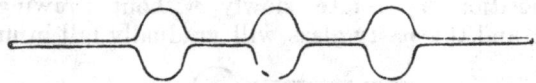

Fig. 121.—Three Bulbs blown on One Tube.

is drawn out to the extent required before the corresponding bulb is blown.

Fig. 122 shows a set of Liebig's potash bulbs, or absorption tubes; these illustrate both forms of bulbs, three

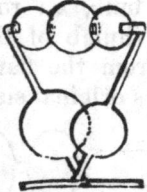

Fig. 122.—Liebig's Potash Bulbs.

of these being made according to the first description, and two others according to the latter. The bulbs are, of course, blown before the tube is bent into shape, its appearance before bending being that of Fig. 123. Other forms of potash bulbs are shown in Figs. 124 to 127.

To prepare an oval bulb, take up a portion of the

½-in. tube in a sloping position, and heat it close to the upper end in the large flame; when sufficiently heated, withdraw the right hand so that a long, fine tube is produced (Fig. 66, p. 42). Seal off this tube. Now bring it

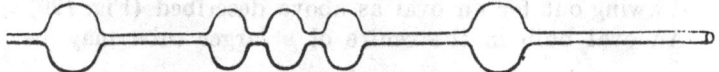

Fig. 123.—Potash Bulbs before being Bent.

again into the flame so that it may be heated at A; again draw out and seal off, when a tube like Fig. 68, p. 42, is produced. Break off one of the points. So far the exercise is similar to the former one.

Rotate the bulb portion of the tube in the large flame, and when thoroughly red hot remove and blow

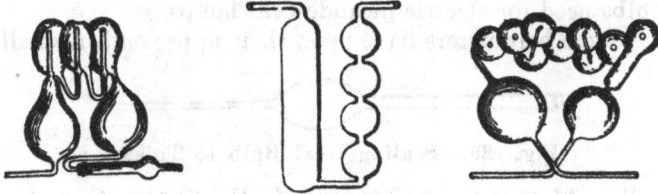

Figs. 124-126.—Potash Bulbs.

gently so as to produce a small bulb. Again get the bulb red hot, withdraw from the flame, and blow gently and continuously so as to produce a large bulb; but as it rises withdraw the left hand, which must now grip the tube, and by this means the bulb is drawn from the spherical shape into an oval (Fig. 128).

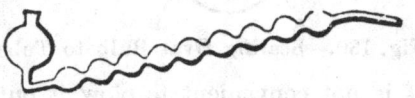

Fig. 127.—Potash Bulbs.

An oval bulb of any size may thus be obtained by regulating the amount of glass used in producing the bulb; for instance, if the size of bulb be increased (Fig. 68, p. 42) by using more of the tube, a larger oval bulb may be obtained in the subsequent operation.

When it is necessary to produce an oval bulb upon the end of a larger tube, after forming the bulb (Fig. 66, p. 42), join it on at A to the tube; then proceed as directed in Chapter IV. for the thistle-funnel bulb, drawing out for an oval as above described (Fig. 129). An oval bulb in the centre of a larger tube may be

Fig. 128.—Making Oval Bulb.

prepared by joining on two tubes, one at A and one at B, and then producing the oval bulb (Fig. 130).

The description of the formation of these bulbs applies, in part, to the manufacture of the small oval bulbs used for electric incandescent lamps.

Some barometers have upon their upper ends a small

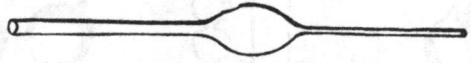

Fig. 129.—Sealing Oval Bulb to Tubes.

bulb. After the exercises given in the first part of this chapter, the blowing of the bulb will be found easy; the length of the tube required must be cut off, and the strong, even bulb blown on the end exactly as previously described.

In producing a bulb upon a tube required for a ther-

Fig. 130.—Sealing Oval Bulb to Tube.

mometer, it is not convenient to blow it out with the mouth, because the moisture which condenses from the breath has afterwards to be removed, and this will be found a somewhat difficult operation. The best plan is to use a set of indiarubber balls like those shown at Fig. 6, p. 12; the tube of the thermometer is connected with these by means of the rubber tube. The heating is carried on just the same as for an ordinary bulb.

In making fractional distillation flasks, suppose that a strong bulb (Fig. 131) has been formed. In order to convert it into a fractional distillation flask, cut a portion of the $\frac{3}{16}$-in. tube about 8 in. long, heat it in the

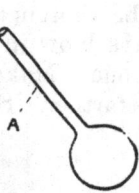

Fig. 131.—Heating Flask to Form Side Tube.

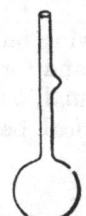

Fig. 132.—Making Flask with Side Tube.

large flame at about 2 in. from one end, draw out and seal. One portion of it will then be about 6 in. long. Heat the bulb tube at the point A with the small flame, blow out slightly (Fig. 132), play upon the tip of this bulb, and then blow sharply so as to burst it. Remove the loose glass; it then appears as in Fig. 133. Now

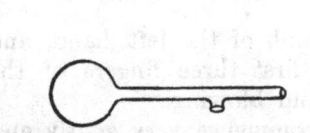

Fig. 133.—Making Flask with Side Tube.

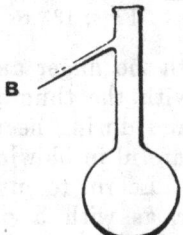

Fig. 134.—Flask with Side Tube.

hold the bulb tube in the left hand, at the same time hold the 6-in. tube in the right hand; bring them into the flame together so that the two openings are heated As soon as the tubes are hot enough, remove from the flame and bring the two openings gently together; blow slightly so as to make the joint good, and then carefully rotate the joint in a small flame. Remove and blow again so as to produce a small bulb, and while the glass is still warm slightly draw out the tube B (Fig. 134), so as to reduce the size of the bulb and make a strong joint. The flask is then complete. Other flasks having side tubes are shown by Figs. 135 to 137.

In blowing bulbs have the tube thoroughly red hot all round, and for large ones always blow in two stages —first, a small one, then a large one. Make the small bulb spherical before proceeding farther. Support the

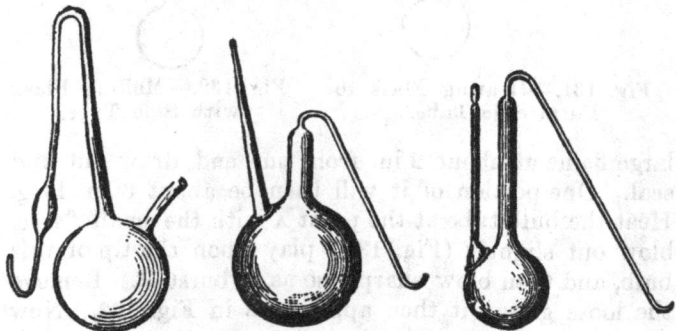

Figs. 135 to 137.—Pasteur's Flasks.

tube with the finger and thumb of the left hand, and rotate with the thumb and first three fingers of the right hand during heating and blowing.

Be careful in blowing to commence very gently and evenly. Learn to use the cheeks as a second air chamber, as with a mouth blowpipe, then gradually increase the force of air as the glass cools. In this way spherical bulbs will be made; otherwise mere balloons of thin glass of various shapes, which burst under the blast, will be produced.

CHAPTER IV.

JOINTING TUBES TO BULBS, ETC.; FORMING THISTLE FUNNELS.

It is often necessary to joint a tube to a bulb, and the method of doing this may be learnt from the following exercise:—Cut a portion of ¼-in. tube 8 in. long, and hold it in a slanting position in the large flame so that one end may be highly heated (Fig. 93, p. 51). As soon as the end seals up and a lump of pasty glass has collected, remove the tube from the flame and blow a

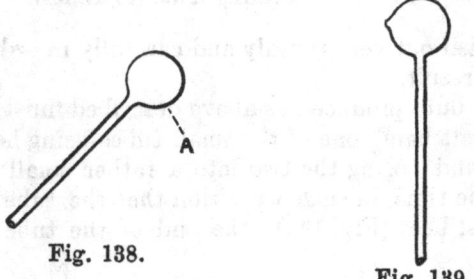

Fig. 138.

Fig. 139.

Figs. 138 and 139.—Sealing Tubes to Bulbs.

small bulb upon the end of it (Fig. 94, p. 51). Now heat the tube at the point shown in the latter illustration, holding it this time horizontally; remove, and blow a second small bulb (Fig. 95, p. 51). Rotate both these bulbs in the flame until they fall together and form one elongated bulb, and then remove and blow a small bulb. Heat again, and then blow out a bulb of about 1½ in. diameter (Fig. 138). Now turn the blowpipe flame low, and with the pointed flame heat the bulb at the point A (Fig. 138) until it becomes red hot. Withdraw the tube quickly, and by blowing quickly burst the bulb (Fig. 139).

Now heat a portion of the $\tfrac{3}{16}$-in. tube 6 in. long, in the centre, draw out and seal off the tube, forming two portions like Fig. 62, p. 41.

It must be borne in mind that a bulb like the one just made is only very thin, and it therefore fuses rapidly. In the ensuing heating the whole process must

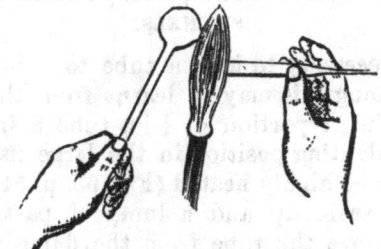

Fig. 140.—Sealing Tube to Bulbs.

be carried out very rapidly and carefully in order to get a good result.

The bulb produced as above described must be taken in the left hand, one of the small tubes being held in the right hand; bring the two into a rather small flame at the same time, in such a position that the tube receives the most heat (Fig. 140); the end of the tube and the

Fig. 141.—Bulb with Tube Attached.   Fig. 142.—Bulb with Tubes Attached.

opening in the bulb are the parts heated. Now bring the two openings together, and blow quickly and lightly so that the glass does not fall in. This is all that is required to make a strong and air-tight joint (Fig. 141).

In order to join on another tube, heat the bulb at the points A; blow out and seal on the second piece of tube (Fig. 142). Receivers made by this method are shown by Figs. 143, 144, and 145.

JOINTING TUBES TO BULBS, ETC. 67

It is necessary to have a small, fine tube penetrating into a bulb or larger tube in the filter pump, and as air traps in barometers, etc.; and in order to produce this

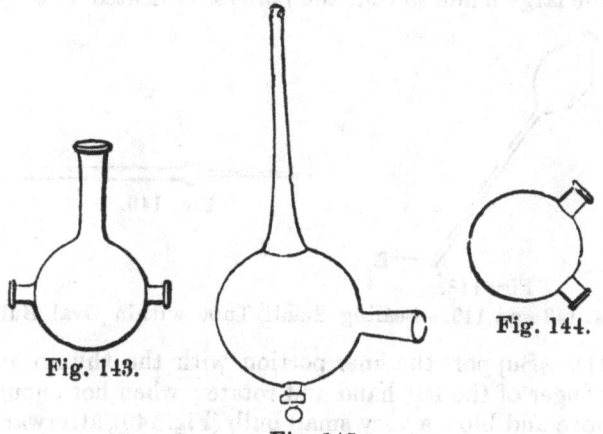

Fig. 143. Fig. 144.

Fig. 145.

Figs. 143 to 145.—Receivers.

an oval bulb is a handy thing to work upon. Take a portion of the $\frac{3}{16}$-in. tube, draw it out in the flame, and seal up the capillary end which is obtained.

Fig. 146.—Sealing Small Tube within Oval Bulb.

Break off one of the ends, and then heat the other fine portion at A (Fig. 128, p. 62); draw away the glass, leaving the bulb as at Fig. 146. Heat the bulb with a

Fig. 147.—Sealing Small Tube within Oval Bulb.

small flame on the point A, and when this part becomes thoroughly red hot, remove and blow out an elongation (Fig. 147). Again heat the extreme end of this elongated part, withdraw, and blow rather strongly so as to burst the bulb, then remove the loose glass, leaving the bulb as in Fig. 148. Seal up the end B and lay the bulb aside for a few moments. Hold the capillary tube in the large flame so that the point A is heated (Fig. 62,

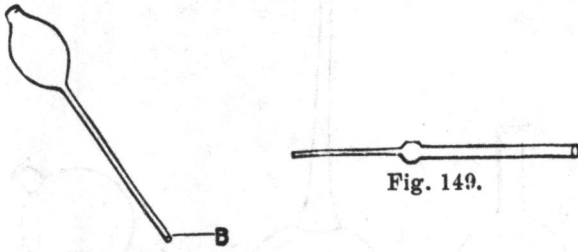

Fig. 148.

Fig. 149.

Figs. 148 and 149.—Sealing Small Tube within Oval Bulb.

p. 41). Support the finer portion with the thumb and forefinger of the left hand and rotate; when hot enough remove and blow a very small bulb (Fig. 149), afterwards cutting the capillary tube so that it is a trifle shorter than the bulb.

Having both tubes ready, take the large bulb tube in

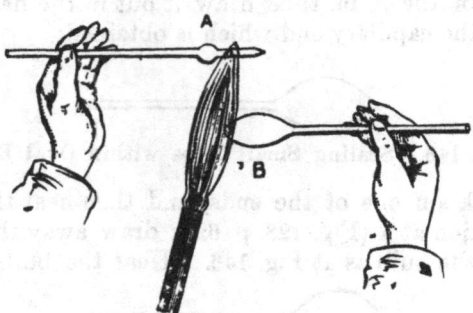

Fig. 150.—Sealing Small Tube within Oval Bulb.

the left hand and the other in the right hand, and rotate them in the edge of the flame so that the points A and B (Fig. 150) are equally heated; they must not become red hot. Having done this, place the tube, A, inside the bulb, B, and rotate them together in a rather small flame, the junction of the two being the part that requires heating; in a short time the tube and bulb become fused together (Fig. 151). To produce a neater and stronger joint, after fusing together remove from the flame and blow gently in at B, and thus produce the result shown in Fig. 152.

It is necessary that the previous exercise should have been mastered before commencing to make a filter pump, in which two tubes within a large tube are required.

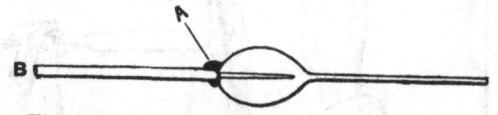

Fig. 151.—Small Tube within Oval Bulb.

First of all, take a portion of the ½-in. tube, hold it in a sloping position in the large flame, and then draw out a capillary portion and seal off as is illustrated in Fig. 66, p. 42; again heat the tube in the large flame at a point, A, about 3 in. or 4 in. lower; again draw out and seal off the tube (Fig. 68, p. 42). Hold a portion of the tube $\frac{5}{16}$ in. diameter and about 8 in. long, in the flame, and draw out to a capillary portion, but not too fine, and then seal it off (Fig. 62, p. 41). Heat

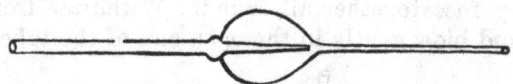

Fig. 152.—Small Tube within Oval Bulb.

this at the point A, and then blow a very small bulb; lay this down and proceed with the next. Draw out another similar portion of the $\frac{3}{16}$-in. tube to a capillary, but not so fine as the last; this may be done by not allowing the glass to become quite so hot. Blow a small bulb upon this tube similarly to the last. Having broken off the end, B, of the first tube, Fig. 68, heat the point, A, with the small flame and draw away the capillary portion, leaving the end as at Fig. 69, p. 42; continue heating this part of the tube, then blow it out into a neatly rounded form, as in Fig. 70, p. 43. Having done this, play the flame upon the extreme end of the rounded part, and then blow vigorously so as to burst it, afterwards removing the loose glass (Fig. 71, p. 42). Sever the finer portion of the third tube made till only about half an inch of it remains (Fig. 153), and then take the

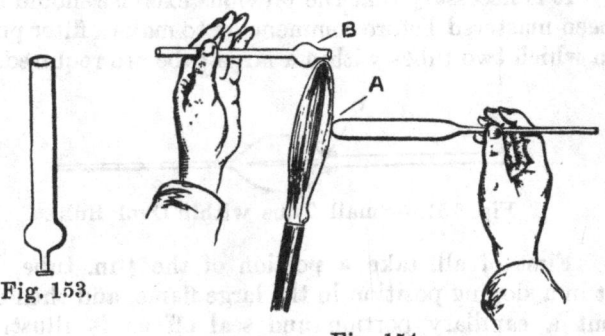

Fig. 153.

Fig. 154.

Figs. 153 and 154.—Making Filter Pump.

first tube again in the left hand, hold the capillary end in the flame for a few seconds till it closes, and turn it round so that the mouth, A (Fig. 154), is warmed; warm the bulb, B, and place it within A heating the junction till they fuse together all round. Withdraw from the flame and blow gently in the open end of the tube, so as

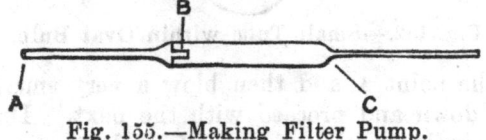

Fig. 155.—Making Filter Pump.

to produce the joint shown at Fig. 155. With the small flame fuse off the fine tube at the point C and heat the end of the tube and blow out into a rounded form; heat up the extreme end, and blow quickly so as to burst this also, afterwards removing the loose glass.

Before sealing on the second tube, fit a small cork to the tube A (Fig. 155). Hold the latter in the left hand

Jointing Tubes to Bulbs, etc.

and take the second tube in the right hand; hold the two in the flame in the same position as Fig. 154 and warm slightly, then place the fine tube within the larger one. Before this is done, the second tube must be cut down with the file so that it will reach just within the mouth of the tube, D (Fig 156). When the junction is fused remove from the flame, and slightly blow out the junction.

Having sealed the two tubes satisfactorily, the side

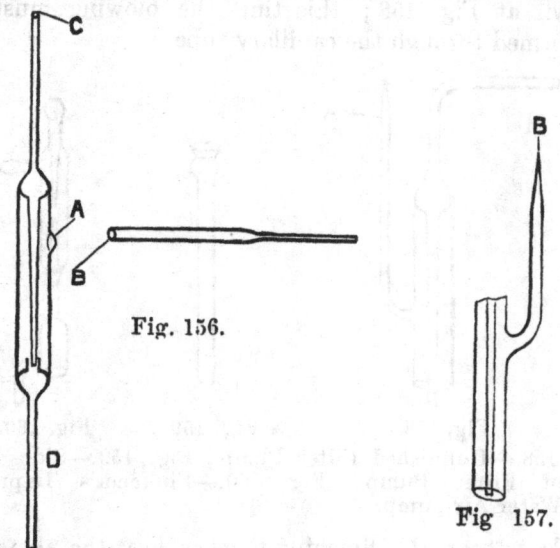

Figs. 156 and 157.—Making Filter Pump.

tube is to be fused in. Draw out a 6-in. length of the ¼-in. tube to a point, and seal off. Take up the filter pump, and with a small flame make it red hot at A (Fig. 156). Blow gently in at the open tube to raise a small bulb; heat the tip of this and blow hard so as to burst it; remove the broken glass. Hold the pump in the left hand with the ¼-in. tube in the right, and place in the flame together. When A and B (Fig. 156) are red hot, bring together gently, rotate in the flame and blow out the junction, then slightly draw down the bulb. Move the pump in the flame so that the side tube, B (Fig. 156), is heated equally throughout a good part of its length, and bend upwards into the position shown at Fig. 157, blowing the while into the open end of the tube, or crumpling will occur. Next break the end of the capillary portion of the tube, B (Fig. 157), and fit a small cork to the tube, C (Fig. 156); heat the latter tube similarly to the last one, and bend down to the position shown at Fig. 158; this time the blowing must be performed through the capillary tube.

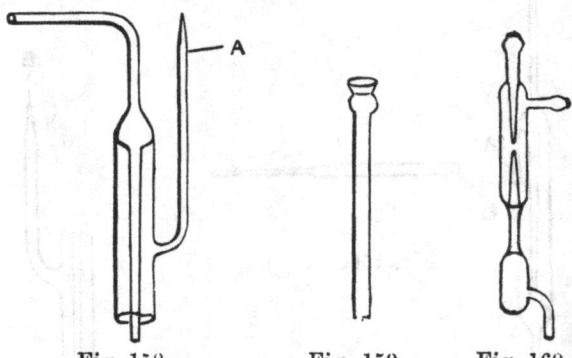

Fig. 158.   Fig. 159.   Fig. 160.

Fig. 158.—Unfinished Filter Pump; Fig. 159.—Side Tube of Filter Pump; Fig. 160.—Finkener's Improved Water Air-pump.

To put on the finishing touches, heat the side tube at the point A (Fig. 158), rotate and very slightly enlarge by blowing; just above this make a file mark on the tube and sever the capillary portion, afterwards holding the open end of the tube in the flame, and opening it out with a piece of stout wire to the shape shown by Fig. 159. The pump will then be complete.

The reason for opening out the end of the tube (Fig. 159) is because the force of water required in working a filter pump is so great that it would jerk the rubber tube off a straight glass tube; therefore the tube is wired between the bulb and the end which is opened out to prevent the rubber tube slipping. In working one of these pumps the side tube is connected to the water-tap, the upper tube being connected to the vessel which requires to be exhausted.

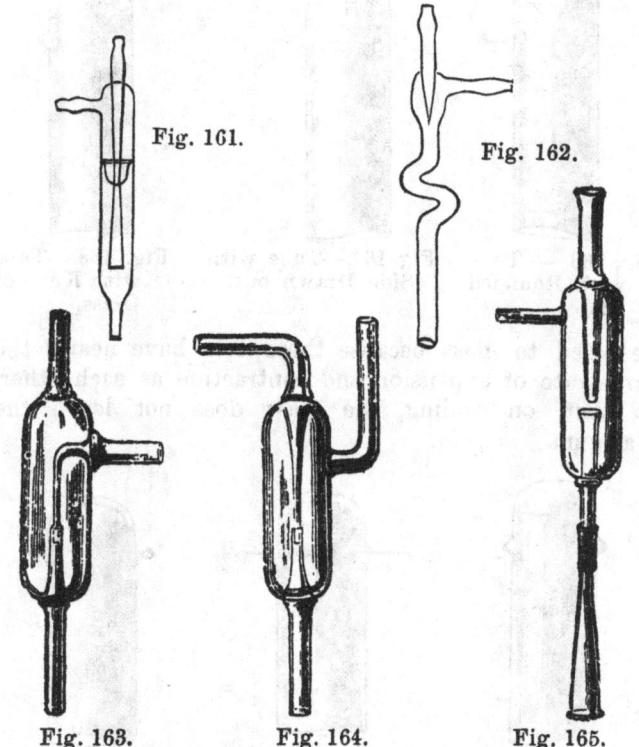

Fig. 161. — Finkener's Water Air-pump; Fig. 162. — Geissler's Water Air-pump; Figs. 163 to 165.—Filter Pumps.

Figs. 160, 161, and 162 show some forms of water vacuum-pumps resembling the filter pump above described. Figs. 163, 164, and 165 are views of filter pumps.

In making an eudiometer, vacuum tube, or glow-lamp it is necessary to seal platinum wires to the glass in such a manner that they shall project both inwards and outwards, and it must be remembered that the joint must be quite air-tight, and be able to stand a vacuum if used for the last two purposes. Platinum wire can

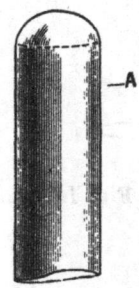 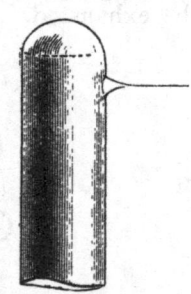 

Fig. 166. — Tube with Rounded End. Fig. 167.—Tube with Side Drawn out. Fig. 168.—Tube with Knob of Glass.

be fused to glass because these two have nearly the same rate of expansion and contraction as each other, so that, on cooling, the glass does not leave the platinum.

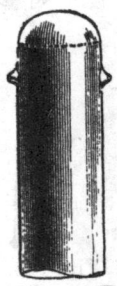  

Fig. 169. — Tube with Knobs of Glass. Fig. 170.—Tube with Platinum Wires Inserted. Fig. 171.—Eudiometer.

Seal up the end of a 12-in. length of ½-in. tube and blow it out so as to get it neatly rounded (Fig. 166).

Take a piece of platinum wire, about ¾ in. long, in the right hand. Hold the tube in the small flame, applying the heat at the point A near the closed end (Fig. 166), on

FORMING THISTLE FUNNELS.

which, when it is thoroughly red hot, place the platinum wire, and quickly draw it away so as to draw out the molten glass, in the manner shown at Fig. 167. Cut the projecting portion with a file to the size (Fig. 168). Now turn the tube round, and heat a point on the other side exactly opposite to the first one; again place the platinum wire upon it, and draw out a second projection; after having been cut, the tube will appear as in Fig. 169. Place a platinum wire in one of the

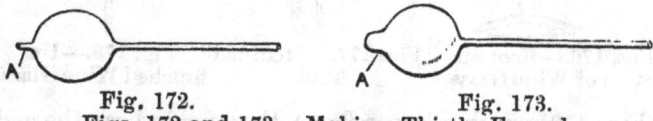

Fig. 172. Fig. 173.
Figs. 172 and 173.—Making Thistle Funnel.

openings, allowing it to project into the tube, almost sufficiently to touch the opposite side. Hold the tube in a small flame so that both glass and wire are heated; the glass will soon melt down until the platinum wire is thoroughly sealed in. Treat the other wire in the same manner (Fig. 170).

To finish off the tube place within it a round stick, having its end rounded off; press this down gently to force the wires to assume the shape of the tube end, but do not use too much pressure, or they will be forced

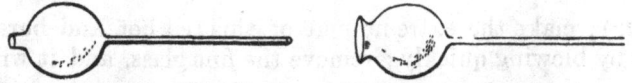

Fig. 174.—Making Thistle Funnel; Fig. 175.—Thistle Funnel.

against the glass. The ends of the two wires should almost touch each other; the stick may then be removed. The wires projecting outside the tube should be twisted round a very small nail to form the loop shown in the eudiometer (Fig. 171). These instruments are graduated after sealing in the wires.

The processes involved in making a thistle funnel will now be considered. Having produced a well-shaped bulb on the centre of a tube, it may be turned into a thistle funnel by the following method:—

76　　　*Glass Working.*

Heat the tube with the small flame at the point A (Fig. 115, p. 58) and draw away the capillary tube

Fig. 176.—Foot and Stem of Wine Glass.　　Fig. 177.—Modified Tool.　　Fig. 178.—Unfinished Wine Glass.

(Fig. 172); with a larger flame thoroughly heat the end of the bulb A, and gently blow out an elongation (Fig.

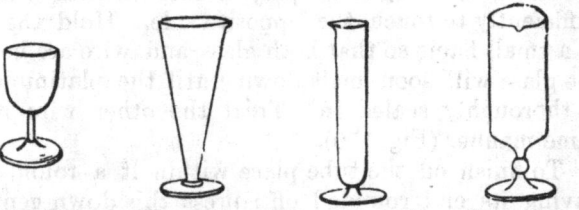

Fig. 179.—Blown Wine Glass.　　Fig. 180.—Test Glass.　　Fig. 181.—Cylindrical Test Glass.　　Fig. 182.—French Test Glass.

173); make the extreme end of this red hot, and burst it by blowing quickly; remove the fine glass, and it will

Fig. 183.　　　Fig. 184.　　　Fig. 185.
Figs. 183 to 185.—Conical Test Glasses.

present the appearance given in Fig. 174. Now turn the flame of the blowpipe full on, and rotate the tube in the flame so that the open mouth is thoroughly heated. The mouth of the tube will lose its sharp outline, the glass fusing and falling in to some extent. Remove the bulb from the flame, place the triangular tool (Fig. 29)

Fig. 186.—Making Funnel

within the mouth of it, inclined at a slight angle, then spin the tube round between the thumb and fingers, gently bringing the mouth of the bulb against the edge of

Fig. 187.—Making Funnel.

the copper tool until it is forced out equally all round, when the thistle head will be complete (Fig. 175). Much practice will be needed for this, and it will be found

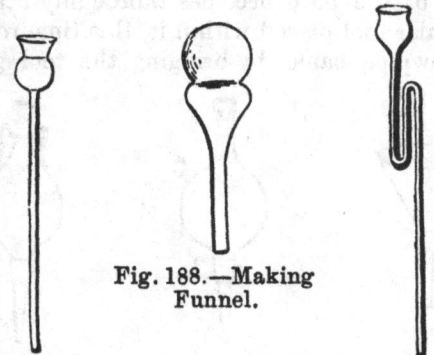

Fig. 188.—Making Funnel.

Fig. 189.—Thistle Funnel.   Fig. 190.—Thistle Funnel with Bent Tube.

that the tendency at first will be to dig the copper tool into the glass, forming a number of inconvenient lips. The mouth of the tube, and that only, must be very hot; the tube must be spun in the left hand almost as smoothly as though it were in a lathe, and the copper tool in the bulb must not be moved, the bulb-tube alone being revolved. Before using the tool, it should be warmed and rubbed with a little beeswax. Thus lubricated, the tool does its work much more easily.

If the thistle head is replaced in the flame so that

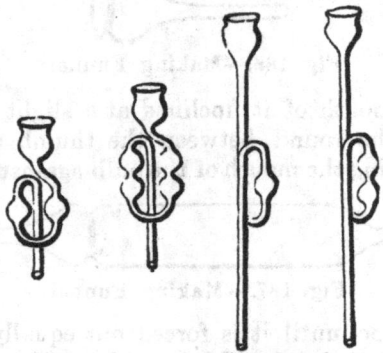

Figs. 191 to 194.—Thistle Funnels with Bulbs.

the whole of the bulb becomes thoroughly heated, and the triangular tool placed within it, this time rotating it in the blowpipe flame by bringing the tool gradually

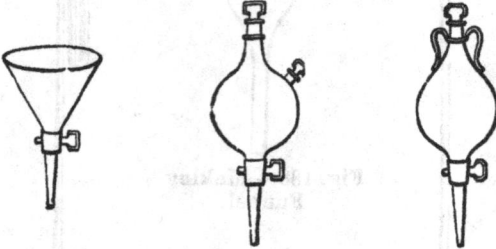

Fig. 195.—Funnel with Stopcock. Fig. 196. Fig. 197.
Figs. 196 and 197.—Separatory Funnels.

down against the glass, it will flatten out into a disc (Fig. 176) like the foot of a wine-glass. It is by this method that the feet of blown glass goods are made.

A somewhat modified triangular tool is seen at Fig. 177; in shape it is half an oval, and is used in making the upper portions of blown glasses. A large bulb is prepared and opened out in a way very similar to the one just described; the bulb is heated and gradually opened out

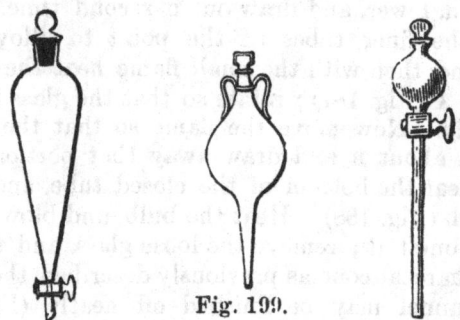

Fig. 198.   Fig. 199.   Fig. 200.
Figs. 198 to 200.—Separatory Funnels.

by using the oval tool until in shape it resembles that of Fig. 178. The foot and head of the wine-glass are each severed from the tubes, and the two joined together

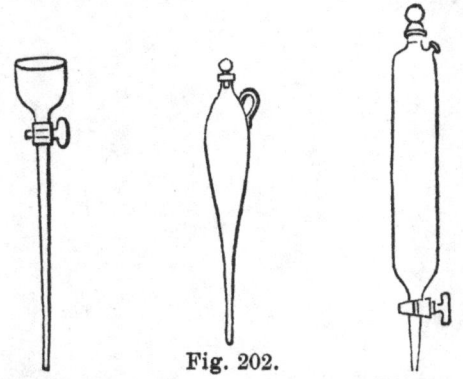

Fig. 201.—Separatory Funnel.   Fig. 202.   Fig. 203.
Figs. 202 and 203.—Separators.

by fusing to a piece of glass rod (Fig. 179). The various glasses illustrated by Figs. 180 to 185 are made on the same principle, though the actual process of course differs in its details.

To form the funnel shown by Fig. 186, heat a piece of ½-in. tube in the blowpipe, and draw one end out as for an ordinary thistle funnel. Again heat the tube about 2 in. lower, and draw out a second time. Break one of the finer tubes at the point to allow air to escape, and then with the small flame heat the tube at the point A (Fig. 187); rotate so that the glass may fall in slightly. Now move the flame so that the tube is heated at about B, and draw away that portion of the tube. Heat the bottom of the closed tube, and blow a small bulb (Fig. 188). Heat the bulb, and blow quickly so as to burst it; remove the loose glass, and then, by using a charcoal cone as previously described, the mouth of the funnel may be finished off neatly (Fig. 186). The remaining half of the tube may be made into another funnel.

Other forms of thistle funnels are shown by Figs. 189 to 194; Fig. 195 illustrates a funnel having a stopcock, whilst Figs. 196 to 203 show various forms of separatory funnels.

CHAPTER V.

BLOWING AND ETCHING FANCY GLASS ARTICLES; GILDING AND EMBOSSING SHEET GLASS.

INSTRUCTIONS have been given in what may be termed the elements of glass blowing, and it is now intended to describe how the preceding exercises, which it is presumed the student has quite mastered, can be turned to account in the formation of fancy articles, such as glass

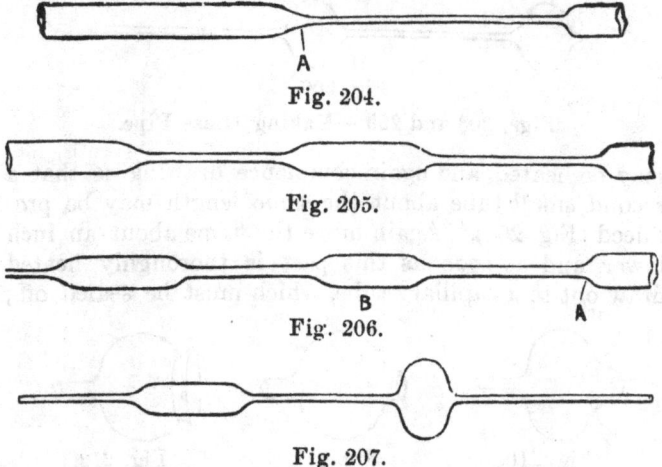

Fig. 204.

Fig. 205.

Fig. 206.

Fig. 207.
Figs. 204 to 207.—Making Glass Pipe.

tobacco pipes and cigarette holders. These, when neatly made, are pretty, but, of course, are not intended for use other than as ornaments.

In making objects of this kind it is the best plan to practise first with plain white glass, and then, when experience has been gained, an artistic appearance can be given by adding coloured glass rod; there is no limit to what can be done with a few differently coloured glass tubes and rod. To make a glass pipe, heat a portion of the

½-in. tube in the large flame so that the upper part may become pasty. As the glass softens gradually, draw away so as to produce a tube about $\tfrac{3}{16}$-in. diameter; while drawing the tube continue rotating, and allow the flame to play upon the wider part, A (Fig. 204). Working in this way for some little time, a tube of fairly equal dimensions, and about 6 in. long, may be obtained. Move the flame so that a portion about an inch lower

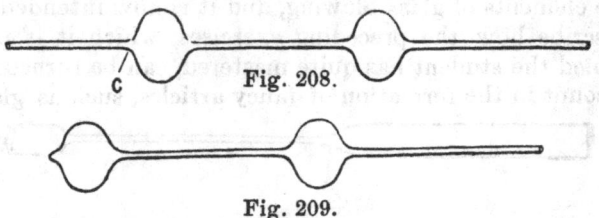

Figs. 208 and 209.—Making Glass Pipe.

may be heated, and again commence drawing so that a second small tube about the same length may be produced (Fig. 205). Again move the flame about an inch lower, and as soon as this part is thoroughly heated draw out to a capillary tube, which must be sealed off;

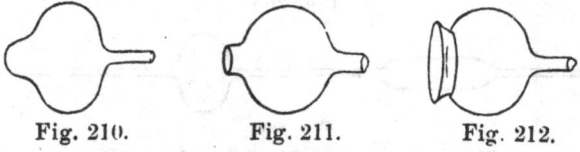

Figs. 210 to 212.—Making Glass Pipe.

then, with a file, sever the upper part at A (Fig. 206). This produces a tube with two small bulbs. Now hold the tube in the flame so that the bulb, B, may be heated, and, supporting it between the two bulbs with the finger and thumb of the left hand, cause it to rotate. When the bulb becomes thoroughly red hot, remove from the flame and blow out to about 1½ in. diameter (Fig. 207).

Having produced the first bulb, hold the second small bulb in the flame. This time the hands are, of course, moved so as to better support the heated portion of the tube; when the bulb becomes red hot, withdraw again from the flame and blow a second bulb somewhat similar to the first one (Fig. 208).

With a small flame heat the capillary portion at c (Fig. 208), draw this portion away, turn up the flame and heat the end of bulb, and blow out the centre into a shape like Fig. 210. Again hold it in the flame so that the extreme end of the elongated portion may be heated, and burst it by quickly blowing (Fig. 211). The tube must now be taken in the left hand, and rotated in the large flame so that the open mouth of the bulb alone

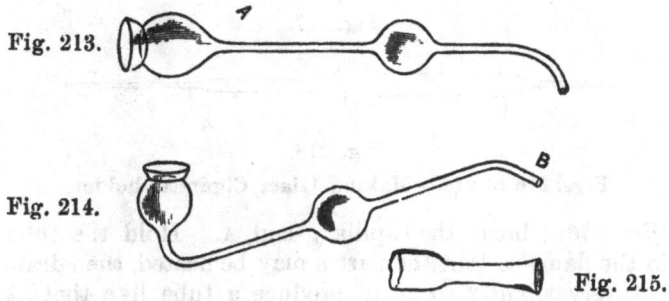

Fig. 213.

Fig. 214.

Fig. 215.

Figs. 213 to 215.—Making Glass Pipe.

is heated. When the open end has become thoroughly red hot, take the triangular tool in the right hand, place it in the open mouth of the bulb, and spin the latter upon it so as to produce the shape shown at Fig. 212.

To finish the pipe, hold it in the flame of a batswing burner, first on one side of the central bulb and then on the other, each time bending very slightly so as to produce the curve shown at Fig. 213. Heat it at the part A, and bend up the thistle head as shown in Fig. 214.

For a mouthpiece, heat the end, B, for a few moments in the blowpipe flame, remove, and give it a cautious nip with a pair of pliers; remove the pliers quickly so that the end may not be unduly cooled. Again heat the extreme tip of the mouthpiece, and slightly flatten it by pressing against it the flat surface of the copper tool. The finished mouthpiece will appear as in Fig. 215.

Another common form of blown glassware is a cigarette holder: in order to produce this, take a portion of the ½-in. tube, draw out to a capillary, and seal off; then, about 4 in. lower, again draw out and seal off

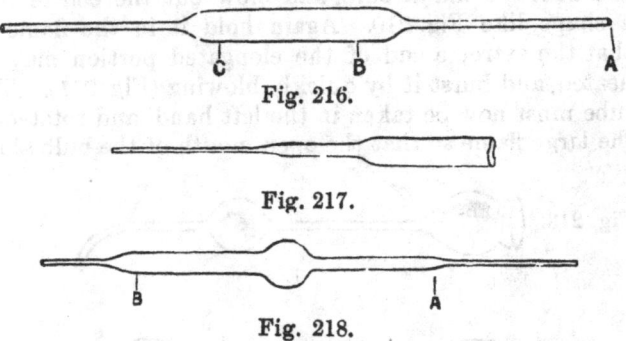

Figs. 216 to 218.—Making Glass Cigarette-holder.

(Fig. 216); break the capillary end, A. Hold the tube in the flame so that the part B may be heated, then draw out very slightly so as to produce a tube like that at Fig. 217. Heat the tube at the part C (Fig. 216), and draw down very slightly, the inner diameter of this tube having to be the size of a cigarette. The bulb

Fig. 219.—Glass Cigarette-holder.

which has been produced must be heated and then blown out to about 1 in. in diameter (Fig. 218), and the capillary ends severed at the marks A and B with the file. The end A may now be heated and pressed with the pliers to form a mouthpiece; the open end is then finished off by again heating, pressing with the pliers, and flattening with the triangular tool as in Fig. 215.

To finish off the end, hold it in a sloping direction

in the flame so that the mouth only is heated, and then open it out (Fig. 219) with a small charcoal cone. As has been before remarked, after skill has been acquired by much practice, coloured glass tubes may be used in making these articles, and ornamentation added by the

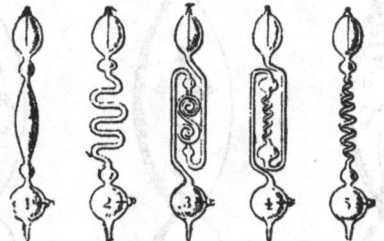

Fig. 220.—Gallenkamp's Vacuum Tubes.

employment of coloured glass rod, portions of which may be fused on wherever fancy may dictate.

Some fine examples of blown glass vacuum tubes are shown by Figs. 220, 221, 222, and 223. In the formation of

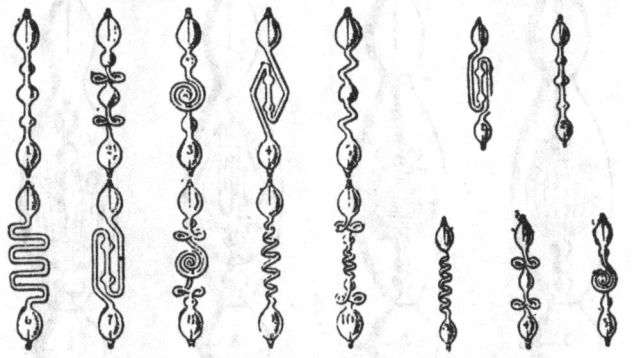

Fig. 221.—Gallenkamp's Vacuum Tubes.

these articles, the various elementary exercises described in detail by Chapters II.—IV. have their application.

Some hints on blowing wine-glasses have been given in Chapter IV., and it is now intended to describe a process whereby wine-glasses and similar glass ware may be etched, and a pleasing decoration so added. A knowledge of drawing and steady practice will be

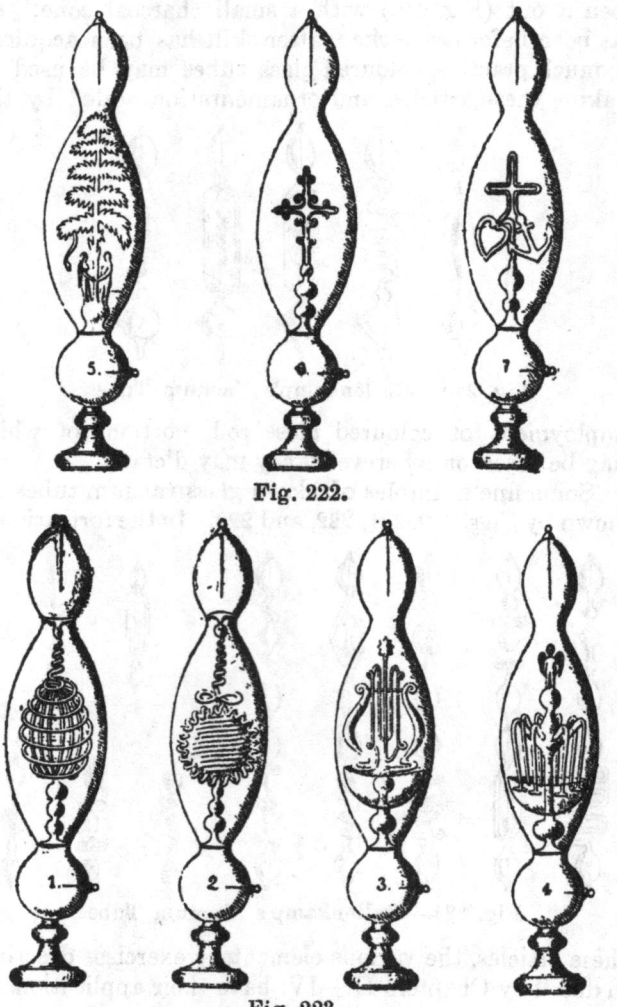

Fig. 222.

Fig. 223.

Figs. 222 and 223.—Gallenkamp's Vacuum Tubes.

required before the information here given can profitably be made use of.

ETCHING FANCY GLASS ARTICLES.

Glass etching may be briefly described as the art of decorating glass by the use of acids, and for this purpose the following materials are necessary:—Pure beeswax, Japan wax, Russian tallow, Swedish pitch, Burgundy pitch, washing soda, soda ash, fluoric acid, sulphuric

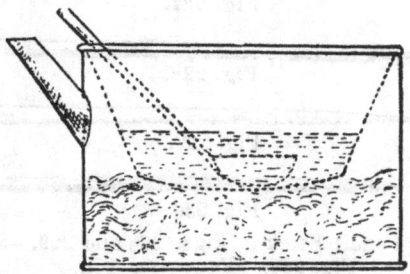

Fig. 224.—Steam Dipping Vat.

acid (best commercial), carbonate of ammonia, powdered French chalk or whiting, dragon's blood, vegetable black, and Brunswick black.

The tools and appliances required are a steam dipping vat (Fig. 224), ladle (Fig. 225), drainer (Fig. 226),

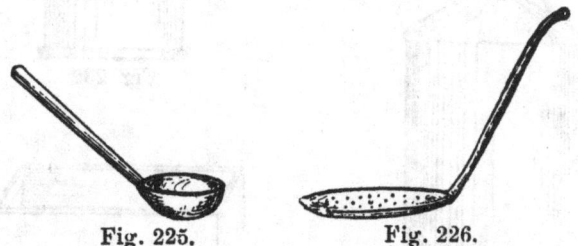

Fig. 225.   Fig. 226.

Fig. 225.—Ladle; Fig. 226.—Drainer.

pencil sticks (Fig. 227), stiletto (Figs. 228 and 229), pouncing pin (Fig. 230), gutta-percha bottle (Fig. 231), and one or two acid vats, also of gutta-percha (Figs. 232 and 233). A small tin or iron saucepan or two will also be needful; those unfit for culinary purposes will do if they are free from cracks or holes.

The dipping vat (Fig. 224) can be made of stout tin,

and a useful size for it will be—the outer pan 12 in. diameter, 9 in. deep; the inner pan 12 in. across the top, 7 in. across the bottom, 6 in. deep. Such a vat would

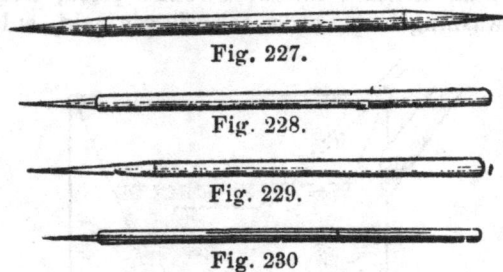

Fig. 227.

Fig. 228.

Fig. 229.

Fig. 230

Fig. 227.—Pencil Stick; Figs. 228 and 229.—Stilettos;
Fig. 230.—Pouncing Pin.

be made by any tinman for 3s. 6d. or 4s. The guttapercha bottle (Fig. 231) and the acid vats (Figs. 232 and 233) can be made any size to suit the convenience of the

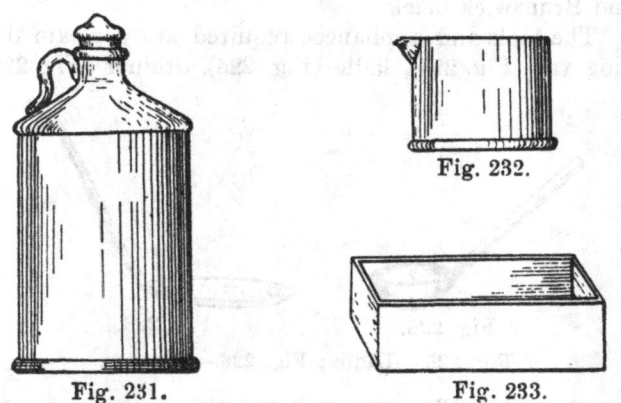

Fig. 231.

Fig. 232.

Fig. 233.

Fig. 231.—Gutta-percha Bottle; Figs. 232 and 233.—Guttapercha Acid-vats.

operator; the round vat may be made with sheet guttapercha ¼-in. thick; large square vats should be made of ½-in. pitch-pine boards with gutta-percha as a lining. The drainer (Fig. 226) is used for dipping tumblers, finger cups, and other articles which cannot be fingered while dipping. To use the drainer, hold it in the left hand, place the tumbler on its edge on the drainer, with the ladle pour over it the resist which has been melted in the steam vat, and, when completely covered, let it drain a little; then carefully slide it off on to the table and let it cool.

For the resist, with which the glass must be coated, either of the following mixtures may be used :—(No. 1) Pure beeswax, 1 lb.; Russian tallow, 12 oz. (No. 2) Pure beeswax 8 oz.; Japan wax, 16 oz.; Russian tallow, 8 oz. (No. 3) Japan wax, 1 lb.; Burgundy pitch, 8 oz.; pure beeswax, 5 oz.; tallow, 1 lb. Melt the resist in the steam vat, wipe the glass quite clean, and place it by the fire or in the oven to get hot

Fig. 234.—Rest for Arm.

evenly all over. It must be as hot as it is possible to handle without burning the fingers. Now, with the glass held by the stem in the left hand, in a slanting position over the steam vat, and with the ladle (Fig. 225) in the right hand, gently pour over the bowl of the wine-glass the hot melting resist—inside first, and outside afterwards—in such a manner as to completely cover the surface. Let it drain a little, and set it aside to cool; this is called dipping. Let the article get quite cold, then with a pad of fine cotton-wool dipped into some powdered French chalk or well-sifted whiting, rub lightly over the coated surface of the glass. This dusting renders the work less trying to the eyes during the progress of drawing the design on the glass.

The necessary tools and materials for this latter part of the work are a lark's quill camel-hair pencil, a cake of Indian ink, pencil sticks (Fig. 227), stiletto (Figs.

228 and 229), pouncing pin (Fig. 230), a little dragon's blood, and some tissue paper. A rest for the arm will also be needed (Fig. 234). The camel-hair pencil is used for rough sketching on the dusted surface merely as a guide before using the pencil sticks or stilettos. The pouncing pin is used for perforating any design in the tissue paper, as shown in Fig. 235. To make a pounce, fold a piece of tissue paper and let the crease be the centre-line of the design it is wished to transfer to the glass. Now draw correctly half of the design the proper size on the folded tissue paper, and, with the pouncing pin, perforate the paper (Fig. 235), being careful to keep to the lines of the design. On opening the paper, the complete

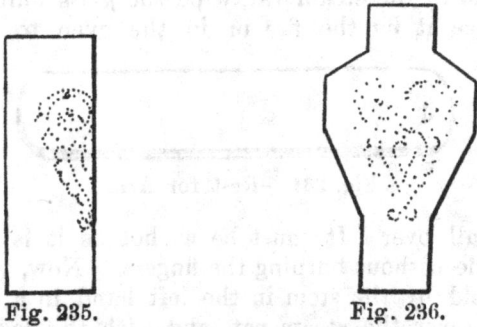

Fig. 235.   Fig. 236.

Figs. 235 and 236.—Perforated Design.

design will be found perforated (Fig. 236). Cut this out, leaving a little margin all round the drawing, as shown in Fig. 236. The pounce is used for transferring any number of the same design, and when used there is no need for the rough sketching with Indian ink.

To use the pounce, place the tissue paper on the glass in a proper position and fix it lightly, but firmly, with two or three small pieces of soft wax, which will adhere to the paper and leave the dusted glass without injury. Dip a small pad of cotton-wool lightly into the dragon's blood, or, if preferred, vegetable black, and rub lightly over the pounce, taking care not to miss any part; the design is by this means transferred to the glass, and forms an excellent guide in the actual drawing of the design on the resist-coated glass. For this, pencil sticks and stilettos are required, according to the coarseness or fineness of the line desired. To make a pencil stick, split a piece of lancewood about 6 in. in length into strips ¼ in. square, and with a sharp knife cut nicely round and point them at each end (Fig. 227). Scrape smooth with a piece of broken glass, and finish with fine glasspaper; harden by well drying.

To make a stiletto (Fig. 228), a piece of soft, close-grained wood (willow is perhaps the best) should be cut to shape. Get a piece of coarse knitting needle, sharpen to a point, and drive it into the end so that it does not split the wood, leaving about ¾ in. of the steel projecting; sharpen this nicely, making the point round and smooth. On no account try to work with a ragged point, as the result will be very unsatisfactory. A bone stiletto can be made by filing off the hook from the end of an ordinary crochet hook; this also will need to be nicely pointed, and will then make a line of medium thickness. A rest for the arm (Fig. 234) can be made with a piece of 7-in. flooring board about 2 ft. 6 in. long; this is attached to the work-table by a stout screw acting as a pivot, so as to move it backwards or forwards as required. For a work-table an ordinary strong kitchen table will be about the right height. It is advisable while at work to sit in the most free and comfortable position possible, for if the operator is in any way stiff or cramped, it will be found difficult to produce good work.

Having made these necessary preparations, the operator may commence the work. Hold the leg of the wine-glass in the left hand and let the edge of the glass rest lightly but firmly against the edge of the table near enough to the rest to allow the right hand to be used with perfect freedom and at the same time to receive such a support from the rest as will insure the making of a nice firm line while drawing on the glass. Take the pencil stick or stiletto in the right hand, holding it as a pencil is held for drawing or writing; let the arm lie on the rest and with the point trace through the resist the design already pounced on the glass. In doing this be sure to bear the pencil stick upon the glass with sufficient weight to remove every trace of the resist and to leave a bright clean surface. If the lines are left greasy from the pencil stick, a broken, rotten line, shown in Fig. 237, will be the result, as the acid only acts where there is no resist.

In choosing the design it is always well to consider with what tools the best effects may be produced. For instance, a bold design may be outlined with a moderately coarse point, and shaded with a fine point, or a neat design may be drawn altogether with a fine point Having drawn the design on the glass, examine it

Fig. 237. Badly Etched Design.

carefully to see if there are any accidental scratches and if so, cover these with a resist made by melting together Russian tallow, 1 lb.; Swedish pitch, 6 oz.; and beeswax, 2 oz. Paint this also on the edge of the glass where the wax has been rubbed off by contact with the bench. Cover also any parts which have not been covered when dipping, and allow to become cold.

Make the etching acid by mixing together fluoric acid, 6 oz.; water, 6 oz.; sulphuric acid, 1 oz. It will be necessary to use a gutta-percha vat for this acid, and, in mixing it, it will be well to place the vat in a small tub or other vessel in which a little cold water has been placed. This will prevent the gutta-percha vat softening by the heat which is generated when mixing the acids and water. Stand the acid vat in the cold water and pour into it the proper quantity of water; measure the fluoric acid and pour this in very carefully a little a a time, and when it is cold (which may be ascertained by feeling the outside of the vat) add the sulphuric acid a little at a time. When cold it is ready for use. To use the acid, pour a sufficient quantity into another vat and immerse the glass in it, weighting it to keep it down. After twenty or thirty minutes take it out carefully and wash with cold water to remove all traces of acid. To remove the resist, sponge with hot soda water; rinse in clean water, and wipe with a soft, clean cloth.

The effect will be a bright, silvery-looking design cut into the glass, and for many designs this is quite sufficient, but for others it is necessary to still further pursue the work by another process, which is called white aciding. The acid for this purpose is made by pouring 1 lb. of fluoric acid into a gutta-percha vat, and dropping into it, a small lump at a time, carbonate of ammonia, until all the latter is dissolved and the effervescence has ceased; it is then ready for use.

To prepare the article for white aciding, fill all the etched lines with Brunswick black by dipping the tip of the finger in the varnish and rubbing over the design in such a manner as to fill the lines and leave as little on the surface of the glass as possible. Set aside for ten or fifteen minutes to dry, then rub quickly over the glass a piece of soft rag damped with turpentine to clean off the black varnish from the surface, and leave the lines perfectly black. Before the scum dries on the glass, breathe on it and wipe over with another clean, soft rag. The glass will then be perfectly clean, and, by placing a piece of white paper inside the glass, the design will be seen in black. Paint carefully round the design and over the whole of the outside and inside of the glass, and when the varnish is dry immerse the glass in the acid so as to completely cover the design. After thirty or forty seconds remove it and dip in clean cold water for a few seconds. Wipe off the deposit, clean off the varnish with turpentine, benzoline, or paraffin, and wash well in hot soda water; rinse in clear water, and finish by wiping on a soft cloth. The earlier stages of the work are shown in Figs. 238 and 239; Fig. 240 shows the glass on completion.

Another white acid may be made by mixing soda ash, 1 lb.; rain-water, ½ gal.; fluoric acid, ½ lb. Dissolve the soda ash in the water, and add the fluoric acid a little at a time; and when the effervescence has ceased let it settle, and it will be ready for use. To use this it is necessary to prepare the glass as for the white acid

Fig. 238.   Fig. 239.   Fig. 240.
Figs. 238 and 239.—Unfinished Etching on Glass; Fig. 240—
Etched Glass Finished.

previously mentioned, but, before putting the glass in this acid, sponge over the design with soap and ordinary soda water. Let it stand in the acid for thirty to forty minutes, and excellent results will be obtained.

When removed from the acid, let the glass stand in clean water until the deposit on it can be sponged off easily. Clean off the varnish as before described.

Do not inhale the fumes from a vat whilst mixing the acids, or while they are being poured in. The acid must be used carefully; never pour unsteadily or handle the acids at random, and avoid splashing. Always wash the hands after using the acids or handling any open vessel containing them. Always keep the different acids in their own vats, or, if circumstances compel the use of a white-acid vat for fluoric acid or *vice versâ*, be sure to rinse the vat well with clean water before so using it. Always keep the acid bottle corked and the vats covered when not in use. Never waste the acids, but when, by use, they get weak and slow in their action, strengthen them by the addition of a small quantity of pure acids —for example, to 6 lb. of weak fluoric acid add 2 lb. of pure fluoric acid and ½ lb. of sulphuric acid. Keep the dipping wax clean by straining it through calico when necessary. Strong soda water, if applied at once, arrests the action of acid on clothing or on the flesh.

It is always necessary to have all articles well and carefully covered with resist before submitting them to the action of the acid, not only the parts which will be immersed in the acid, but those parts which may be exposed to its fumes. This will prevent sulphuring, and so keep all plain parts of the glass clear and bright.

The following instructions, if carefully followed, will enable sheet glass to be tastefully embossed and gilded at a very low cost.

The design should be drawn upon a sheet of paper the size of the glass, after which the paper is oiled so that the design may show clearly on the other side. The paper is then laid face downwards on a flat surface, and, the glass having been carefully cleaned, is laid face downwards on the paper, edge to edge. The design in reverse should be clearly seen through the glass. With a red sable pencil and Brunswick black carefully draw on the glass an outline of the design, after which those portions of the glass not to be embossed should be covered with the black. The Brunswick black must flow freely, dry quickly, and cover with a thin film to resist acid. When dry, remove the paper pattern, and to protect it from the fumes of the acid, well oil the face of the glass; lay it perfectly flat as before, with its face downwards, and build a wall of wax or tallow about ¾ in. high all round the edges so as to form a tray or tank. Into this tray a solution of one part fluoric acid to two parts water is poured, and allowed to remain for from twenty to thirty minutes; it is then poured off and the glass thoroughly cleaned preparatory to gilding.

The size for gilding is made by gently boiling one dram of isinglass in a quart of water and straining; the other requisites are a gilder's tip, knife, cushion, and gold leaf. The paper pattern and the glass are again arranged as at first, but, instead of horizontally, at an inclination of about 45°; if the glass is very large it should be set upright, the pattern being kept in place in any way that is convenient. The parts to be gilded should receive a liberal application of size, which may be allowed to overflow down the glass. Gold leaf is then applied wherever it is required, and the glass is set aside for several hours until perfectly dry, when, in the case of special work, it may be "second laid," or gilded a second time. "Mounting and Framing Pictures," a companion handbook to this, contains full instructions on gold-leaf gilding, and should be consulted to make this part of the process intelligible. The gilding, when perfectly dry, can be brightened by washing with hot water and a flat camel-hair brush. Again remove the paper from the glass, and perforate with a needle point the lines of the pattern in such a way that when it is reversed upon the gilded surface of the glass the design may be pounced with chalk or whiting; afterwards fill in with a backing colour composed of white-lead, red-lead, and gold size (in equal proportions), or quick varnish. The surplus gold unprotected by a backing can be brushed away with a damp, clean brush. The gilding is now finished. If there are letters in the design, any shading or blocking must be written backwards in the chosen colours. When all is dry the final background colours are laid on and allowed to dry hard.

CHAPTER VI.

UTILISING BROKEN GLASS APPARATUS: BORING AND RIVETING GLASS.

IN this chapter it is intended to show how the stock of more or less broken apparatus, which is acquired by every experimentalist and glass blower after a time, can be mended or converted into other useful articles.

A test-tube is often broken or cracked at the mouth (Fig. 241). To mend it, make an ink-mark straight round the tube below the cracked or broken portion; then, by means of a pointed and heated glass rod, lead the crack on to and then round the ink-mark. If a crack has not

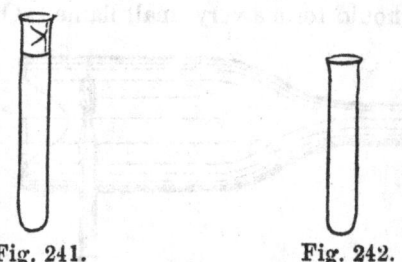

Fig. 241.   Fig. 242.

Fig. 241.—Cracked Test-tube; Fig. 242.—Test-tube mended at Mouth.

already started, make a notch with a file and place the heated glass rod upon the notch, from which a crack will immediately proceed. Finish off the mouth of the tube by heating it in the blowpipe flame, and using the charcoal cone, as directed in making test-tubes (see p. 40). Fig. 242 shows the appearance of the tube with its mouth re-made. If the tube is a wide one it may be cut by using a hard steel point on the inside, as shown in Fig. 243. With a little practice it can be made to scratch a perfect circle, when the piece can be easily broken off.

Another way of cutting a tube or bottle (the latter is shown in Fig. 244) is to draw out in the blowpipe flame a piece of glass tube so that it forms a fine nipple, and

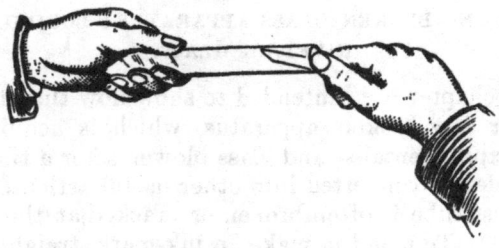

Fig. 243.—Cutting Wide Test-tube.

connect this by means of rubber tube with the gas supply; when the gas is turned on and lighted at the nipple it should form a very small flame. Or a plumber's

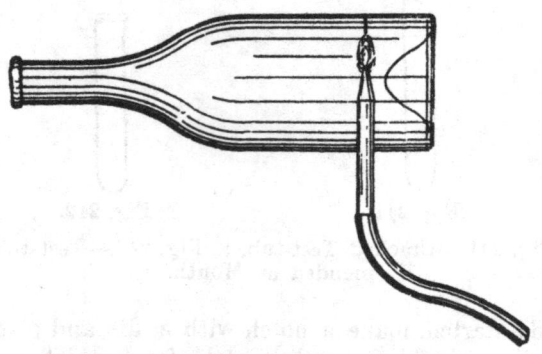

Fig. 244.—Cutting Glass Bottle.

blowpipe could be used instead. With a pen and ink mark the tube or bottle where the cut is to be made, and then make a deep file mark on this ring, and apply the flame to it. After a few moments the flame may be removed, and a drop of water placed on the spot; a crack usually forms, but, if not, the process is repeated.

Or a crack may be started by a slight tap with a hammer. Now move the flame in front of the crack, which will travel round: Fig. 244 gives an idea as to how this is done. At the last eighth of an inch, the part may be lifted off easily. To mark the bottle fill it with water to the desired line and place it on a level

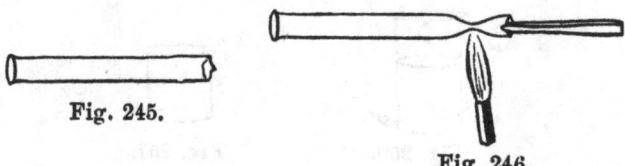

Fig. 245.

Fig. 246.

Fig. 245.—Broken Test-tube; Fig. 246.—Resealing Test-tube.

table, then, the surface of the water acting as a guide, draw an ink line around.

If the bottom of a test-tube is broken (Fig. 245), heat it in the blowpipe flame (Fig. 246), hold a piece of glass rod at the same time in the flame, and when both

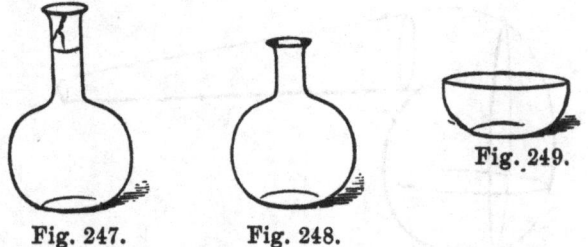

Fig. 247. Fig. 248.

Fig. 247.—Cracked Flask; Fig. 248.—Flask mended at Neck; Fig. 249.—Dish made from Flask.

are red hot bring them together; when they adhere, draw away the glass from the tube until it is sealed, then draw away the superfluous glass and finish off as before directed.

It is most probable that this will not be neatly done except after experience has been gained; but even if the tubes will not do as test-tubes again, corks may be fitted to them, and they will do to hold small quantities of chemicals, etc.

If a flask is cracked at the neck (Fig. 247), lead the crack round, and afterwards remake the neck by heating and using the charcoal cone (see Fig. 248).

It very often happens that a flask is cracked so that

Fig. 250.—Cracked Beaker ; Fig. 251.—Beaker Re-made.

it cannot be used again. By leading the crack around the side or bottom, very useful dishes may be made (Fig. 249). The edges of these dishes need filing very carefully on both sides, or they will most surely crack either on heating or cooling. If the bottom of the flask is sound, then a flat cover-glass may be got out of it.

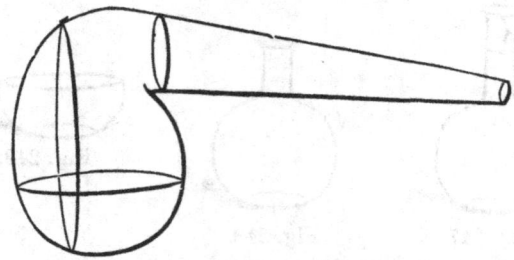

Fig. 252.—Retort Cut for Dishes.

A beaker that is cracked at the mouth (Fig. 250) may be cut down, the sharp edges filed, and used again (Fig. 251); if it is too much broken for this, a cover-glass may be cut from the bottom of it.

Cracked beakers are also very useful for covering specimens, in the same manner as the broken wine-glasses used for covering parts of watchwork.

A retort is a useful apparatus even when broken, as

from it many other articles may easily be made. At Fig. 252 is shown a method of cutting out two shapes of glass dishes from a retort body. One shape is oval and the other round.

The neck of a retort may be used as an adapter (Fig. 253), for joining a retort to a receiver where extra length of cooling surface is required.

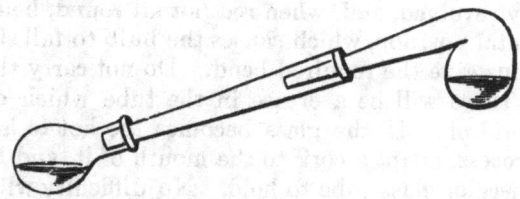

Fig. 253.—Adapter.

Another form of adapter may also be made by drawing down the neck of the retort in the blowpipe flame to a tube about 12 in. long, which is then bent, and the mouth of the tube finished off with the charcoal cone.

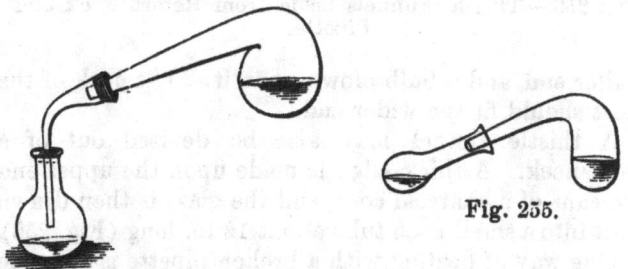

Fig. 254.
Fig. 255.
Fig. 254.—Adapter; Fig. 255.—Improvised Retort and Receiver.

It serves to connect the retort and flask in a very neat manner (Fig. 254).

Retort necks may also be used to make smaller retorts and receivers, as shown at Fig. 255.

For the retort, the neck must first be fused up at its larger end in the large flame of the blowpipe, a glass rod being heated at the same time. The rod is then brought on to the neck at one side, and when it has thoroughly adhered, the hot glass is drawn towards the other side until the two sides of the neck adhere and fuse together. The heat is now moved up the tube a little, the tube revolved, the superfluous glass drawn away, and a slight bulb blown upon the end (Fig. 255).

The heat is now further moved up the tube, the tube quickly revolved, and, when red hot all round, held in a horizontal position, which causes the bulb to fall slightly and thus give the required bend. Do not carry this too far, or there will be a crease in the tube which cannot be got rid of. If the glass becomes too hot to hold in this process, adapt a cork to the mouth of it, and have a long piece of glass tube to hold. No difficulty will then be found.

For the receiver, another tube is sealed up at its

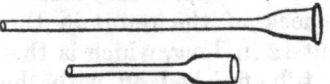

Fig. 256.—Thistle Funnels made from Retort Neck and Pipette.

smaller end, and a bulb blown upon it. The neck of the retort should fit the wider end.

A thistle funnel may also be devised out of a retort neck. A thick edge is made upon the upper end by means of a charcoal cone, and the glass is then drawn down into a small even tube about 12 in. long (Fig. 256).

One way of dealing with a broken pipette is to make it into a thistle funnel (Fig. 256).

Broken bottles may be made use of. If the bottle is a large round one, and broken at the neck, cut the neck off, so as to leave an even edge, file down the edge, and make for it a neat cardboard lid; it may then be used as a jar for storing such material as rice, etc. (see Fig. 257).

A small broken bottle cut down and provided with a pasteboard lid does very well for storing dry substances.

UTILISING BROKEN GLASS APPARATUS. 103

A large wide-mouth jar, with the bottom cut out, as at Fig. 258, makes a very good deflagrating jar, which need not be taken from the pneumatic trough when the burning body is introduced.

Small bottles that are broken at the neck may

Fig. 257.—Jar made from Bottle.

be cut down and used to hold stirrers, pipettes, or test-tubes.

It is sometimes necessary when repairing apparatus to bore a hole in brittle and extremely hard glass. This is an operation that requires much care; otherwise, the risk of cracking the glass is very great.

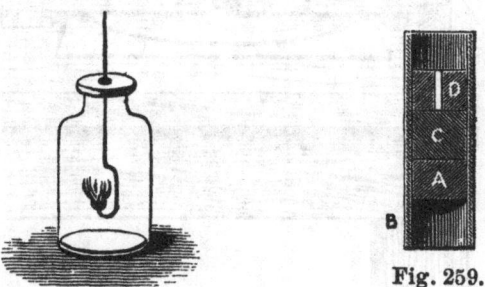

Fig. 258.

Fig. 259.

Fig. 258.—Deflagrating Jar; Fig. 259.—Copper Tube for Boring Glass.

Below are given a few methods of boring holes, and they may be relied upon as being the outcome of practical tests.

In order to drill a hole in glass, it is necessary to have a hard and well-tempered steel drill. This may be made by heating to a dull red, and then plunging into mercury so as to become hard. It is, however, necessary to temper the shaft of the drill. Imbed the point of the drill in a piece of lead. The temperature of the shaft of the drill can be raised by means of a blow-

Fig. 260.—Boring Holes in Glass.

pipe till there is a blue colour nearly to the point. The drill and lead together are now immersed in cold water, when the former will be ready for work. This drill, when mounted in a holder and the point moistened with turpentine, attacks glass rapidly. Do not press too heavily when working the drill, and, if possible, drill from both sides successively. To enlarge a hole thus obtained, use a rat-tail file soaked in turpentine.

Any steel drill may be hardened, when at a red heat, by dipping it into any cold liquid. A spear-shaped drill heated to a red heat and hardened in mercury and then sharpened on an oilstone may be used. Still another method is to forge a drill at a low temperature and harden it in salt-water. The drill is firmly rotated at the desired spot with an alternate motion, and lubricated with a saturated solution of camphor and spirits of turpentine. Dilute sulphuric acid has also been used as a lubricant.

To drill a hole of a larger diameter, the edge of a copper or brass tube, the outside diameter of which equals the diameter of the required hole, must be kept revolving on the proper spot while being supplied with turpentine and grain emery. Some precautions are necessary to insure the glass from breakage.

To mount the tube, drive a wood block, A (Fig. 259), past the centre of the copper tube, B (Figs. 259 and 260), to be used tight enough to turn it. On this lay a piece of indiarubber, C, and above that fit in another piece of wood, D, with a hole in centre. This hole is for receiving a three- or four-cornered reamer, or other suitable tool, fixed in the drill brace, in order to rotate the tube. The indiarubber between the blocks of wood gives the necessary amount of elasticity, without which the glass would be broken. During the process of boring, only press very lightly on the tool.

It will be found necessary to guide the tube by special means, as it is difficult to keep it revolving in the one groove—a block of wood, as illustrated, raised on two pieces of wood, whose thickness depends on the work to be drilled. To form a guide, a hole equal to the outside diameter of the copper tube, B, is bored in the block (this, in Fig. 260, is shown broken), which is fixed at each end either by cramps or screws. The glass, laid on several thicknesses of paper, is placed in position under the drill.

Nails placed round the glass keep it in place, or it may be pressed down by means of wood wedges inserted between the block of wood and the glass.

A very simple tool for boring glass is a drill made by heating an old three-cornered file, which is then

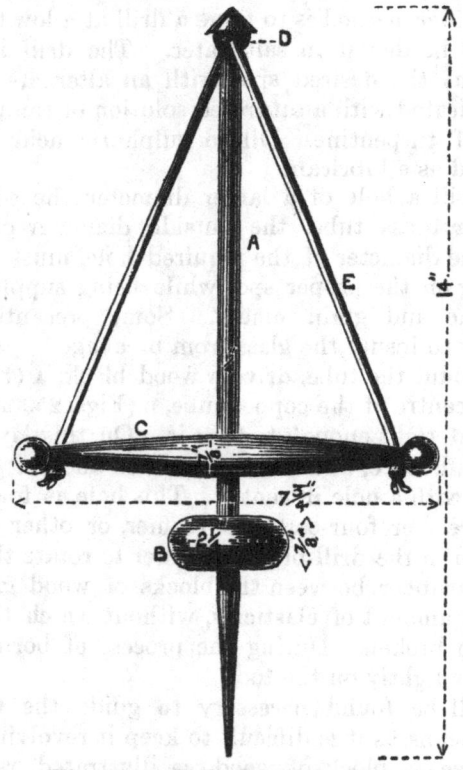

Fig. 261.—Drill Stock for Glass.

cooled slowly in ashes. The end is filed to a conical shape and again heated, and then hardened by plunging into water. The drill is fixed in a brace and rotated, turpentine being used as a lubricant. To remove the tool from the hole, rotate it in the reverse way.

Another method of drilling holes, in which a tube is used, is as follows:—Make a drill from brass tube of the required diameter and into the non-cutting end drive a piece of wire to project somewhat, and file the projecting part to fit a drill-stock. The cutting end of the brass tube is next to be slotted with a few sawcuts running parallel with the tube's length; the inner ends of the cuts must terminate in holes drilled, before the slots are cut, at right angles to the tube's length. The number of slots required depends upon the diameter of the tube used. Two pieces of wood measuring, say, 3 in. wide, ¾ in. thick, and long enough to span the piece of glass in hand, are screwed firmly together, with ordinary wood screws passing through near the ends, whilst through both pieces of wood a hole is bored large enough to freely admit the drill. This hole through the wood is to be countersunk at both ends. The two pieces of wood are next separated, by partly removing the screws, and the glass is placed between them and held as in a kind of clamp, the hole for the drill being brought exactly over the spot where the glass is to be bored. Some 90 or 120 grade emery powder mixed with water is then placed in the countersinking to act as a grinding agent. The drill may be worked as fast as possible, though not so quickly as to splash out the wet emery. When the drill is half-way through the glass from one side, a hole should be started from the other side and completed, to prevent the chipping of the edges. Holes from ⅛ in. to 2 in. in diameter can be made with this appliance. It takes about four minutes by this method to make holes up to ½-in. diameter in a sheet of glass ⅛ in. thick.

Still another method is to employ a diamond bit, but this will be dealt with in the instructions on riveting glass now to be given.

The materials required for riveting glass are few and simple. A drill, some diamond bits, a pair of combined cutting and holding nippers, some brass wire, and a little plaster-of-Paris are all that are necessary. The drill stock (Fig. 261) may be bought ready made, but it can easily be constructed in accordance with the following instructions:—Obtain a steel spindle A (Fig. 261), 14 in. long and ¼ in. diameter. One end should be tapered; the other should be slightly flattened and have a hole, D, drilled through it to take the tape E. Turn up a piece of hardwood, such as box or ebony, to 7¾ in. long and ⅞ in. thick; C (Fig. 261) shows its shape. Drill a hole through its centre of a diameter large enough to allow it to slip freely up and down the spindle. Pass the latter through this finger-piece; a heavy flywheel of the shape shown at B, having a hole through its centre, should

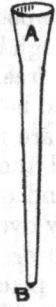

Fig. 262.—Diamond Drill Bit.

then be hammered on over the tapered end for 1¾ in. or so, to make a tight fit. Tie a piece of tape or a leather lace to one end of the finger piece, or pass it through a hole, which may be drilled in the end, and knot it underneath. The tape is then threaded through the hole D in the spindle and fastened to the other end of the finger-piece, and the drill is complete.

The drill-bits or drill-tubes, one of which is illustrated by Fig. 262, are pieces of tin or copper twisted into a somewhat conical shape. Each tube must have an opening at its base large enough to freely admit a diamond spark and to allow of the edges of the tube being securely closed with the pliers round the diamond. The sides of these tubes are parallel for ½ in. or so from the lower end; it will be found necessary to have a supply of drill-bits of different sizes for thin, medium, or coarse ware. To efficiently set a diamond in a drill-tube requires some practice.

The wire for the rivets is usually of brass, though other metals may with advantage be used in some cases; for flint or light-coloured glass it is usual to employ white metal, tinned brass, or even silver, all of these being less noticeable than brass. The wire should be of from 12 to 16 B.W.G., and should be flat on one side; it may be easily made so by scraping with an old knife or by filing.

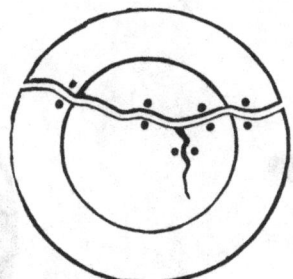

Fig. 263.—Plate Drilled for Riveting.

It is supposed that a glass or china plate (Fig. 263), having a part broken off and containing also a crack, requires to be riveted. Clean the broken edges of all grease and dirt, bring them together, and, as it is advisable that the rivets should be placed in that part of the plate not much seen when it is afterwards in use, turn it bottom upward. Now mark with dots of ink the places where the rivet holes are to go, on both sides of the break and crack. It is usual to bore the holes at a distance of ¼ in. from the break, but, in cases where much strain will come upon the rivets, ⅓ in. and even ½ in. should be allowed. It is essential that the holes on either side of a break or crack should be exactly opposite each other, so that the rivets cross the crack at right angles to it; otherwise the action of the rivets will tend to draw the broken edges out of their true positions.

Fasten an appropriate-sized bit to the drill stock, and, having first insured a good starting-point for the diamond by scratching away the glaze from the ware

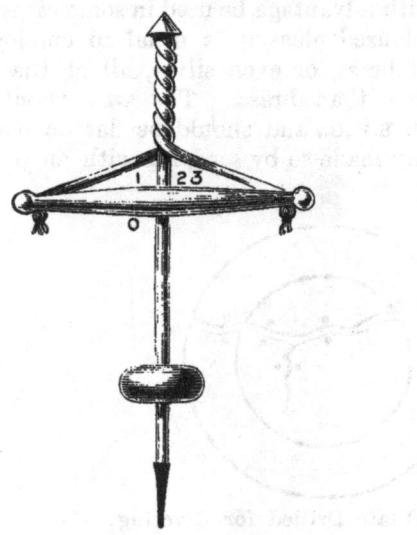
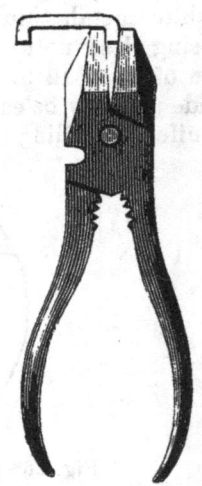

Fig. 264.—Drill with Tape Twisted.

Fig. 265.—Nippers for Bending Wire.

with a steel point, grasp the wooden finger-piece of the drill with the thumb and first finger on the left side of the central spindle, and the second and third fingers on the other side; twist the tape round the rod as in Fig. 264, give a slight downward pressure to the finger-piece, when the tape will uncoil, and, by raising the hand at the proper moment, it will recoil in the opposite direction. The numbers in Fig. 264 refer to the position of the fingers when using the finger-piece. Practice alone will enable the worker to obtain a rapid and continuous motion. It would be as well if some little time were spent in practising upon a piece of wood with the drill stock without the bit. Drill as deeply as the article will allow, using as a lubricant either camphorated oil, turpentine, or a solution of one part of camphor in five parts of turpentine.

Finish drilling all the holes before proceeding to make the rivets. These are made by taking a piece of the prepared wire and, by means of the nippers, turning down at right angles one end about $\frac{1}{15}$ in. or $\frac{1}{8}$ in., according to the depth of the holes already bored; the flat side of the wire should be kept underneath, and, to get the bend of the right shape, the wire should be lightly tapped with a hammer whilst held in the nippers (see Fig. 265). Hook the wire in one hole, carefully mark where the bend ought to come, allow for the little piece to be turned down, and then cut off and turn down by means of the nippers. Gentle tapping with a hammer may be necessary to make the rivets go right home into the holes, but care should be taken that the edges of the ware are not thereby chipped. See that neither of the turned-down ends is so long that it prevents the rivets lying flat. Mix a little plaster-of-Paris with water, and fill up the holes around the rivets, wiping off the surplus plaster whilst it is still damp.

It is sometimes desirable to adopt a stronger form of riveting, or to give additional strength to a joint already riveted in the ordinary manner, and recourse is then had to a method known as "through and through" riveting. This consists of boring the holes right through the ware instead of only partly so, as has been just described. Fine binding wire, of the kind used by florists, is then laced in and out through the holes, and is finished off by twisting the ends together, and may then be cleaned, polished, and soldered over. It is often necessary to smooth down, by means of a file, any little roughness, especially where the wire has been twisted and soldered.

In some cases of breakage it is impossible to employ rivets, and cement is then made to serve the purpose. A cement joint is inferior to one skilfully made with rivets, but, for all that, a properly cemented joint may last for years with careful handling. Cements suitable for the purpose are the following :—

(1) Place a small quantity of glue just covered with water in a wide-mouthed bottle, and allow to stand for twelve hours; then pour off the excess of water and cover the glue with methylated spirit. The bottle is then placed in a pan of water and heated until the glue is melted, then a little whiting is shaken into it, the bottle removed from the pan, cooled, and tightly corked. Sometimes a small piece of gum mastic, together with some ammoniacum, is added to such cements.

(2) Cover gelatine with strong acetic acid, and, after standing, melt it down by placing the bottle in hot water, and then allow time to cool. This and cement No. 1 are ready for use after placing for a few minutes in hot water.

(3) Silicate of soda or potash (commonly known as water glass) sticks well to glass, and will stand heat. Either the potash or soda silicate, however, attacks and slightly roughens the glass.

(4) A heat-resisting cement for glass is made by pulverising together in a mortar ½ oz. of powdered glass and 1 oz. of fluorspar until they are reduced to an impalpable powder; this is then mixed with 3 oz. of silicate of soda and worked into a smooth paste. This paste must be applied immediately it is made, as it sets very rapidly.

The edges of the glass should be thoroughly cleaned before applying the cement, and in the case of cement, 1 and 2 should be warmed also.

CHAPTER VII.

HAND-WORKING OF TELESCOPE SPECULA.

THE most representative process of shaping glass by abrasion is, perhaps, speculum working; and it is on that account that a short treatise on the hand-working of telescope specula is included in this handbook. It must be distinctly understood that speculum working differs in every respect from those methods of shaping glass which have already been described and in which the softening of the material by the aid of heat has such an extensive application. Indeed, in the processes

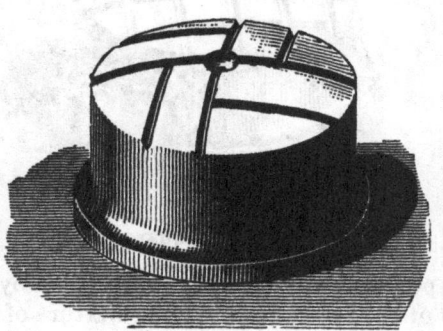

Fig. 266.—Convex Tool.

now to be described, any heating much above the ordinary air temperature is to be avoided, as otherwise the speculum may be distorted.

As the simplest way of conveying a general idea of the process of speculum making, the method followed by the old workers in metal may be considered, the modern method of working being identical in principle with that of the seventeenth century. In the centre of the workshop stood a small bench, or barrel, of such a size that the workman could walk quite round it, and reach over to every part of it without effort. In the centre of this bench was placed the first convex tool (Fig. 266), formed of the same metal as the speculum. Moistened emery was spread on this tool, and the concave metal was worked in every direction over it, until the surface was sufficiently true and smooth. The furrows in the tool, and the little central depression, allowed the abrading material to circulate freely and to cut evenly.

A second tool (Fig. 267), made of small squares of hone arranged on a convex base, was then substituted for the first, and with this the speculum was finely ground

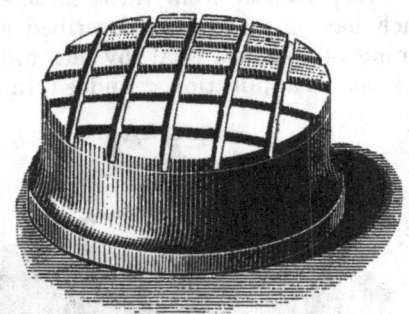

Fig. 267.—Hone Squares Tool.

ready for polishing. A polisher was formed by covering the facets of the second tool with a mixture of pitch and resin, and on this the speculum was polished with rouge. During the last process the concave mirror had imparted to it the parabolic curve necessary to obtain good definition in a telescope.

The operator, during the whole time of working, walked ceaselessly round and round the bench, changing the line of movement of the inverted speculum at each stroke, and to alter the curve of the speculum he altered the length or variety of the stroke with which he moved it to and fro over the tool or polisher. He knew from experience the effect caused by any such change of stroke, and in this knowledge lay his skill.

HAND-WORKING OF TELESCOPE SPECULA. 115

Now the practical optician still works his glass specula on convex metal tools, and still polishes them on pitch. But the tool of hones, and the metal tools also, may be dispensed with, and two similar discs of polished plate glass will be used ; one to ultimately form the speculum, the other to be the tool. The

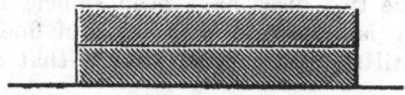

Fig. 268.—Glass Discs together.

glass tool is covered with pitch, and on it the speculum will be polished with rouge, thus dispensing with the metal tools. If two flat discs of glass be placed one over the other, with emery between them, and the upper disc be pressed down and worked to and fro in every

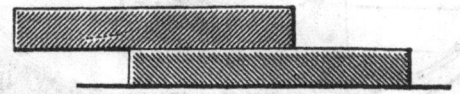

Fig. 269.—Overhanging Glass Disc.

direction over the lower, the emery will cut away the centre of the upper and the edge of the lower disc.

The two discs, as illustrated in Fig. 268, are at rest. However, at the end of a stroke, as shown in Fig. 269, the upper disc overhargs the lower, the centre of the

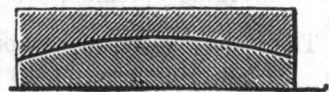

Fig. 270.—Curved Section of Glass Discs.

one pressing on the edge of the other, and the tendency is to wear away the two surfaces, and produce the curved section shown in Fig. 270.

Fig 271 further explains the working. The tool is cemented to a wooden slab, and then screwed to the rigid bench, and the speculum, with a handle cemented to its back, is worked to and fro in such a manner that no two consecutive strokes are in the same direction. Thus the concavity in the upper disc is cut regularly. As the workman walks round he causes the speculum to rotate slightly under his hands at each stroke. The necessary muscular action comes easy and natural with a little practice.

When the two discs have been sufficiently shaped, the grinding is continued with series of finer grades of emeries, until the glass is so smooth that emery can

Fig. 271.—Working Speculum over Tool.

do no more. Then the polishing is completed with rouge on pitch. It can thus be seen that the process of hand-working in the nineteenth century is practically dentical with that in the seventeenth century.

The following materials must be provided before work can be commenced :—(a) Two discs of polished plate glass. (b) A curve gauge to indicate when the glass has been made sufficiently concave. (c) Sand or grain-emery for rough grinding. (d) Flour-emery of various grades for fine grinding. (e) Rouge (peroxide of iron) for polishing. (f) Pitch.

HAND WORKING OF TELESCOPE SPECULA. 117

The instructions here given apply especially to making a speculum 5½ in. in diameter, and 5 ft. in focal length. The principle of construction, however, applies to specula either larger or smaller, and both the diameter or the focal length mentioned may be altered at will. Anyone who is prepared to overcome extra difficulty may reduce the focal length even to 3 ft. A speculum of large diameter is not recommended for a first experiment.

Two discs of polished plate glass, each 5½ in in

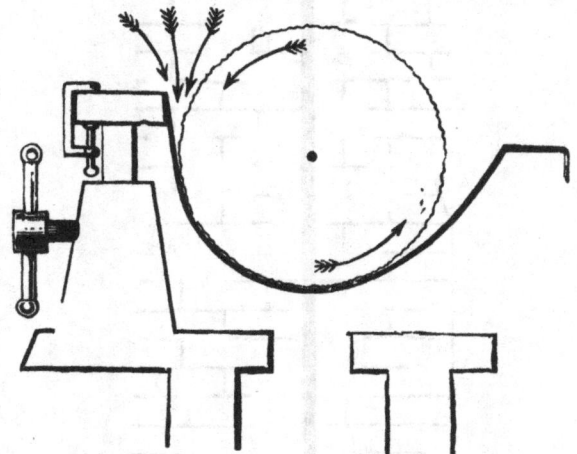

Fig. 272.—Edging Glass Disc in Lathe.

diameter and 1 in. in thickness, may be obtained from a glass merchant with the edges either rough or ground smooth. The price with rough edges should not exceed 1s. 6d. for each disc, and the charge for smoothing the edges would probably be a like amount.

The edges of the rough glass may be smoothed on a large grindstone, using plenty of water, or they may be mounted in the lathe and cut true with emery, which is more workmanlike. A disc of wood is cemented to each face of the glass, which, thus mounted, is chucked on the lathe. The bearings and exposed parts of the lathe must be shielded from any emery which may be

118 GLASS WORKING.

thrown off by the rotation of the glass. A strip of soft sheet iron, bent as in Fig. 272, is secured to the slide-rest so as to spring against the revolving glass. The lathe is

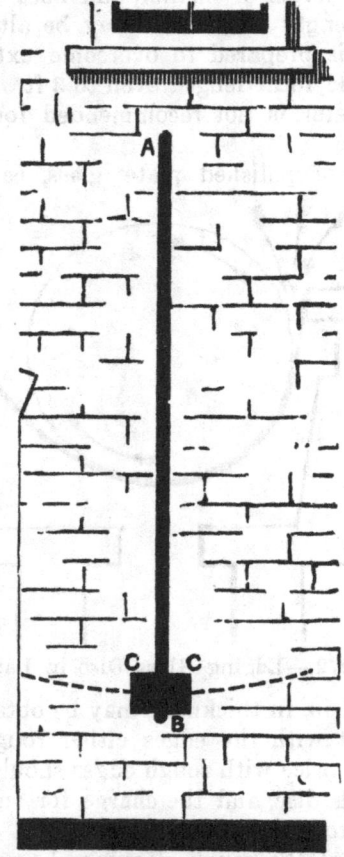

Fig. 273.—Radius Bar on Wall.

then driven at slow speed, and grain-emery (or quartzose sand) and water is fed in the direction of the arrows, until the glass is reduced to shape by abrasion. Flour-emery is then used for a short time, until the surface is suitably smooth. The coarse emery may be received in

HAND-WORKING OF TELESCOPE SPECULA.

a saucer placed on the bed of the lathe, and so used again and again. The time necessary to edge a 5½-in. disc is about three hours.

To avoid the risk of emery grains lodging in the notches of the jagged edge of the disc intended for the tool, this also should have its edge smoothed.

The focal length of a concave speculum for parallel

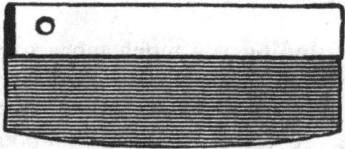

Fig. 274.—Convex Metal Curve-gauge.

light rays (as in a telescope) is one-half the radius of its curvature. As the speculum is to be of 5 ft. focal length, the radius of its curvature must be 10 ft.

Take a lath of a greater length than 10 ft., and so fix it by one end that the other end may swing free (as in Fig. 273). Ten feet distant from the pivot, A, insert a sharp-pointed tool, capable of cutting through the plate

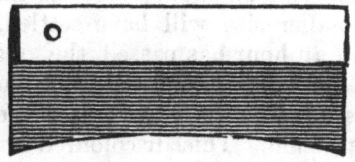

Fig. 275.—Concave Metal Curve-gauge.

of sheet zinc or copper, C, C. By repeatedly moving the rod to and fro, the sheet of metal is cut through, and forms two templates or curve gauges, the one convex (Fig. 274), the other concave (Fig. 275), the curved edges of which should be smoothed to fit perfectly, and edge of the straight part turned back, as shown, to secure rigidity. If it is not convenient to swing the radius bar on a wall, the curves may be cut on a level floor.

Either grain-emery or sharp sand may be used for the first roughing out. Ordinary silver sand is less expensive than emery, but it loses its cutting power more quickly than the latter does. Coarse emery is named according to the number of meshes in each square inch of the sieve through which it has passed in manufacture. Forty, sixty, and ninety hole emeries are suitable for the rough grinding and the first smoothing of the glass.

The fine grinding is a much more exact process, for which flour-emery is used after it has been separated into several grades by the process of elutriation now to be described. A vessel containing about two gallons of water has poured into it a pound or more of good flour-emery, and the mixture is well stirred. Good flour-emery is of a bright chocolate colour. Powder of a slaty hue is probably adulterated, and possesses insufficient cutting power. Care bestowed on the process of elutriation is likely to be amply rewarded. The coarser grains at once sink to the bottom, but a quantity of finer powder remains in suspension. If the mixture be left entirely undisturbed, at the end of ten seconds all the grains above a certain size will have settled to the bottom. At the end of twenty seconds all the grains of a certain smaller size will have settled, and so on, until, when half an hour has passed, the greater mass of the emery will have fallen, and only the finest particles of it, visible as a slight discoloration in the water, will remain in suspension. This discoloured water is carefully poured or syphoned into a clean, shallow vessel, and allowed to stand aside, carefully screened from dust, until the fine powder which it contains has been precipitated. The quite clean water is then drawn or syphoned off, and the powder which is left adhering to the shallow vessel is dried and collected.

The original mixture being again stirred, and again allowed to subside, the water, charged with powder, is drawn off at the end of fifteen minutes, and the powder collected as before, the process being five or six times repeated in some such order as that indicated in the following table :—

Finest grade *a* collected after 30 minutes' suspension.

b	,,	,,	15	,,	,,
c	,,	,,	6	,,	,,
d	,,	,,	2	,,	,,
e	,,	,,	1	,,	,,

Coarsest grade *f* ,,   ,, 15 seconds' ,,

The coarser grains, which will not remain in suspension for fifteen seconds, should be used only for preliminary smoothing.

The table of times, and consequently the degrees of gradation, vary with different opticians. That cited above was used by a famous lens-maker.

Other tables of eminent workmen are :—

Ross, *a* (finest) 60 minutes' suspension.

b	,,	20	,,	,,
c	,,	10	,,	,,
d	,,	2	,,	,,
e	,,	30 seconds'		,,
f (coarsest)	10	,,		,,

Draper, *a* (finest) 30 minutes' suspension.

b	,,	10	,,	,,
c	,,	3	,,	,,
d	,,	1	,,	,,
e	,,	20 seconds'		,,
f (coarsest)	3	,,		,,

It will be observed that the finest powder is necessarily drawn away first, and the coarsest last. In the successive drawings of water the greatest care is needed to prevent any disturbance of the coarser sediment. Of the finer grades a very small quantity will be obtainable from a pound of flour-emery, and but a very small quantity is required. To complete a 5½-in. speculum, not more of the finest grade will be necessary than could be contained on a sixpenny piece. It is best to use for the elutriation earthenware or glass vessels. The powder adheres to the enamelled surface, and, after drying, can be rubbed with the finger tip into a little heap and collected with ease. Each grade of the washed emery should be kept in a separate labelled bottle or box.

The rouge used is not that sold as toilet powder, but is the peroxide of iron specially prepared, and known commercially as jeweller's rouge. It is of a colour varying from deep red to red with a decided purple tinge, and the latter is the best quality. An ounce is sufficient to polish several specula.

Pitch is used as a cement, and to form the polisher; it can be purchased, of suitable quality, from any chemist. When cementing glass to wood, or glass to glass, the surfaces should be always first slightly warmed, that the hot pitch may not be chilled by contact.

The tool being fastened to the centre of the bench (Fig. 271), the shaping of the concavity may be attempted. A handful of wetted sand, or a lesser quantity of coarse grain emery, should be spread evenly on the tool, and over this the speculum should be pressed down and moved to and fro with long, swinging, deliberate strokes, the greatest care being taken that the centres of tool and speculum coincide at each stroke. The workman should also move slowly round the bench, in order that no two consecutive strokes may be given in the same direction. Water must be freely used, and in no circumstance should dryness be allowed. When it is felt that the sand or emery no longer cuts, it may be washed off with a sponge and fresh abrading material supplied. The centre of the speculum and the edge of the tool will first become deeply scratched, and then actually worn away, but the grinding must be continued until the concavity of the speculum fits the convex metal gauge (Fig. 274, p. 119), which should be applied vertically and diametrically. The rough cutting of the concavity of a 5½-in. speculum should be completed in from four to five hours. It is better that the curve should be a little too deep than too flat, for it will flatten slightly in the first stages of the fine grinding.

HAND-WORKING OF TELESCOPE SPECULA.

After the rough grinding is completed, the glass and the bench must be carefully cleaned. The presence of a stray grain of coarse emery or sand during the later working might be disastrous, therefore it is best to use a quite fresh sponge for the finer processes.

The desired final curve is given to the speculum by judiciously varying the length and direction of the movement of the speculum over the tool, and the skill of the workman lies almost entirely in a knowledge, gained by experience, of the exact effect of any given variety of stroke on the concave surface.

A long, swinging, straight stroke has been found best to cut away the centre of the speculum, and so it fol-

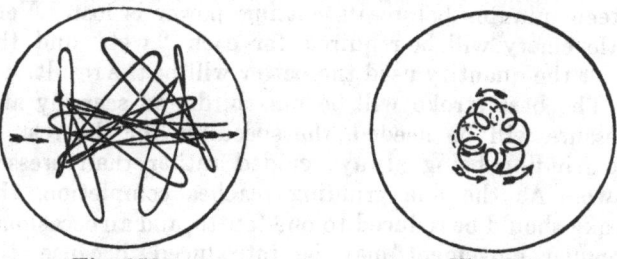

Fig. 276.   Fig. 277.
Figs. 276 and 277.—Diagrams showing Path of Speculum.

lows that a shorter stroke will cut away the surface more evenly; the latter is therefore adopted, generally, throughout the fine grinding.

A straight stroke of one-third or one-fourth of the diameter of the speculum will tend to equalise the wear and keep the concavity spherical. Any greater stroke will tend to deepen, and any lesser stroke will tend to flatten, the curve. But it is desirable at intervals to work for a short time with an irregular stroke, in which the centre of the speculum wanders erratically from the centre of the tool. Such a stroke is illustrated in Fig. 276, which is the reduction of a tracing from a Rosse machine. The short curved stroke, which will be hereafter referred to, is illustrated by Fig. 277, which shows the path of the centre of the speculum over the tool.

With this knowledge the fine grinding may be proceeded with. The roughly cut surface of the glass has to be smoothed by working with the successive finer grades of emery powder. Unwashed flour emery may be used until the glass presents a fairly uniform appearance — that is, until the coarse scratches or pits left by the sand have almost disappeared. Then the graded emeries must be employed.

The object of each successive grade is to reduce the scratches of the preceding grade, and thus the workman decides, by examination, when the time has arrived to change any given grade for the next finer. A "wet" of well-prepared, good emery should work for from ten to fifteen minutes before its cutting power is lost. Very little emery will be required for each "wet," and the lesser the quantity used the better will be the result.

The best stroke will be one-third, and scarcely any pressure will be needed, the speculum for the rest of the grinding being always guided rather than pressed down. As the fine grinding reaches completion, the stroke should be reduced to one-fourth, and an occasional irregular movement may be introduced, because the danger of working the concavity out of centre will have passed.

In the actual process, emery is wetted to the consistency of cream, and carefully spread over the tool, the tip of the finger being used to detect and remove grit. The speculum is then placed centrally over all, and at once pressed down hard in order to crush any large grains which may have escaped notice. Two or three short circular strokes are then given to distribute the abrading material, and then straight strokes are maintained, the wetted emery being felt distinctly to cut the glass. The chocolate colour of the emery slowly changes to grey as the fine glass becomes incorporated with it. The sensation of cutting ceases, and finally the speculum moves as on stiff grease. It is then slid (not lifted) from the tool, and the glass surfaces cleaned before fresh emery is applied.

From lack of skill the centre of the concavity may, in the rough grinding, be cut too deeply. If this be so, it will become evident when the finer working is begun, because, while the greater part of the glass will be perceptibly smoothed, the central depression will remain rough. In such a case it is best to return to the coarser grinding for a short time, and work with an irregular stroke and without pressure.

It is desirable to test the focal length before the graded emeries are brought into use. This is effected by wetting the smoothed glass surface and placing it in the direct sunlight so that it will reflect a faint image of the sun on to a shaded paper or wall. When the reflected image is smallest the distance from mirror to the image will be the approximate focal length. If it be found to be too long or too short, it can be most speedily corrected by rough grinding, using a long, straight stroke to shorten the focus, and a short, circular stroke to lengthen it.

Assuming that the focus is correct, the fine grinding may now be steadily proceeded with, using the graded emeries in careful succession from the coarsest to the finest, and doing the utmost that can be done with any one grade before the next finer is applied. With the three finest grades it is a good plan, at the end of ten or fifteen minutes' work, to slide the speculum off and wash it, leaving the tool unwashed, and then to return and work the wet speculum over the unwashed tool for five minutes longer. This secures a very delicate surface. It is not necessary, when changing emery, to dry either the speculum or the tool, and drops of water, may, of course, be applied at any time as required.

When fine grinding has been properly performed, the final curve is quite spherical, and the surface of the glass is semi-transparent, appearing as if covered with a film of dried milk. It is then ready for polishing.

The finely-ground glass surface is polished with rouge, carried on a pad formed of pitch, which easily assumes and temporarily retains any desired curve.

The glass tool must be covered with a ¼ in. coat of pure black pitch, faceted as in Fig. 278, in order that the surface may be free to expand, and that the moisture which carries the rouge may easily circulate. It is better to arrange the facets so that the centre of the central facet does not coincide with the centre of the tool, or a short, straight stroke may cause the speculum to be polished in rings. Fig. 279 shows a method of arrangement adopted after exhaustive experiments with polishers of many shapes. By such an arrangement a great part of the polishing can be safely done with straight strokes, a decided advantage to an inexperienced workman. The

Fig. 278.—Facets of Pitch on Glass Surface.

white spot in the centre of Fig. 279 indicates the centre of the glass tool.

One method only of forming the facets need be given. Fig. 280 shows a little tool formed of three pieces of wood screwed together. The blades, A, A, should be about ⅛ in. thick, and very slightly bevelled at the lower edge, which edge should be of the same curve as the metal gauge (Fig. 274, p. 119). The centre-piece B needs to be of the same width as the facets, about ⅜ in. The facets are stamped out by pressing the little tool, wetted to prevent adhesion, on to the warm pitch.

Pitch, as obtained from the chemist, is practically free from grit; but if any doubt exist as to its purity, it may be strained through a sieve of distended muslin. It is safest to melt pitch in an oven and in an earthenware vessel. If it be allowed to boil, air bubbles will form and destroy the homogeneity

Hand-working of Telescope Specula. 127

All things being ready, lukewarm water in a bowl, sufficiently large to permit the speculum to be immersed, should be placed near to hand, together with the stamping tool. A strip of stout paper, wetted with rouge and water, should be fastened round the edge of the glass tool, so as to form a rim about ¼ in. high, and thus prevent the liquid pitch from flowing off. The tool being then carefully dried and slightly warmed, the pitch may be poured; it will spread slowly and cover all the sur-

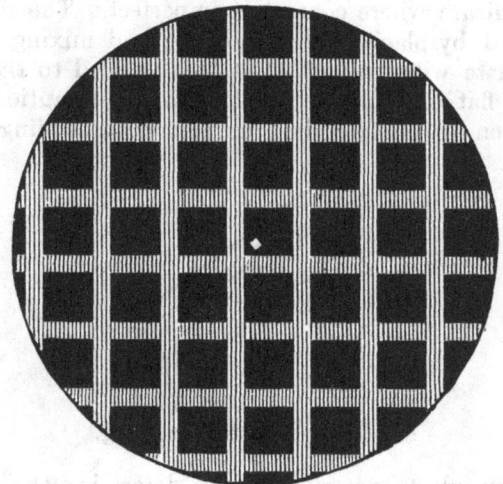

Fig. 279.—Faceted Glass Tool.

face, and should be immediately shaped to proper thickness by the aid of the wetted speculum, the stamper being used to form the facets as speedily as possible. If necessary, the pitch may be warmed again and again, but not sufficiently to cause it to run.

In practice it will be found that facets moulded by a stamper will present a slightly concave surface. This may be remedied by bevelling their edges with a sharp chisel or an old razor, and then shaping the whole surface again, after warming, by the aid of the wetted speculum. The greatest care must be taken not to allow the speculum to dry, and so adhere to the pitch, and for this reason its position should be constantly altered a little, and rouge and water mixed should be used for the damping, instead of water only.

Finally, the facets having been trimmed square and regular, the paper rim and any superfluous pitch should be neatly cut away. A properly prepared polisher should be everywhere in contact with the speculum. To test this, paint the facets separately with rouge, and apply lightly the clean, dry speculum. The imprint will indicate where contact is imperfect. The rouge is prepared by placing it in a bottle and mixing it to a thin paste with water. It is best applied to the pitch with a flat camel's-hair brush. Every precaution must be taken to prevent dust or grit from settling on it.

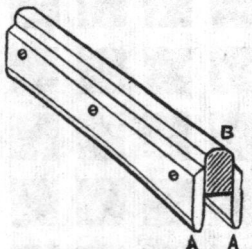

Fig. 230.—Tool for Faceting.

It is difficult to describe how to determine the proper hardness of the pitch, but it will be speedily perceived if it be too yielding or too rigid. When cold, a moderate pressure with the nail should indent it. The pitch purchased from a chemist is commonly of a quite suitable consistency. To soften pitch, add oil of turpentine; to harden it, add resin.

The remaining processes are polishing and figuring. The term "polishing" is self-explanatory; "figuring" is the process by which the polished surface is given the necessary parabolic curve. The processes may be combined or performed separately. The former course was that pursued by the old workers, and needs a wide experience. In the latter course, the spherical curve possessed by the smoothed glass is maintained unaltered until polish is complete, and is then deliberately changed to the parabola, the work being carried out under the guidance of the Foucault shadow test, to be described later.

The first method will now be noticed. Let it be borne in mind that a spherical mirror can be made parabolic and perfect for the telescope either by deepening the curve regularly from edge to centre, or by flattening the curve regularly from centre to edge.

The fine grinding, if it has been properly performed, leaves the prepared speculum spherical. Polishing is proceeded with, using short (one-third to one-fourth) straight strokes, the direction of each stroke being, of course, carefully varied, and an occasional irregularity being introduced. As the polish approaches completion, the stroke is changed to a very short curve, the edge of the speculum overpassing the edge of the tool but very slightly. This flattens the curve from centre to edge, and thus parabolises it. At the close the straight stroke is again, for a very short time, reverted to.

The result may be successful, but the success or failure depends on knowledge, only to be gained by experience, of the length of time for which each variety of stroke should be used. If unsuccessful, the Foucault method of testing, to be described later, will indicate where the imperfection lies; the curve must, of course, be corrected.

The second, a more scientific method, is that which should be followed by an inexperienced worker. The same short straight stroke is used, with slight variation, until the polish appears. It will then be perceived that abrasion is taking place equally on the whole surface, or in excess either at the edge or at the centre—most probably the latter. The stroke is accordingly maintained or modified, as it is found that the wear is equal, or more at the centre than at the edge, or *vice versâ*. The object is to determine, by a little slow experiment, the exact stroke which will distribute the polish equally. The work should then be steadily continued until the polish is sufficient to permit the shadow test to be applied.

After a speculum is quite polished on the large polisher, it is sometimes discovered, under test, that some particular narrow zone of the surface needs reducing, and that this cannot be easily accomplished on the main polisher without endangering the rest of the otherwise perfect curve. In such a case the speculum is laid face upwards on the bench, and a very small polisher of faceted pitch, formed on a base of turned wood, is moved with spiral stroke over and over the faulty zone until enough of the glass is cut away. This "local polishing" is advocated by some experienced speculum polishers and deprecated by others.

The spherical curve with which the glass leaves the tool at the close of the fine grinding is sometimes mechanically deepened to the parabola by the use of a shaped polisher. The ordinary square facets are gradually and very slightly diminished in width from the centre to the edge, so that the abrasion, with a stroke which would otherwise secure uniform action, becomes greatest at the centre and least at the edge. The same principle applies when the spherical curve is flattened to the parabola by the use of a polisher rather larger than the speculum, so that, instead of equal wear, the abrasion is greatest at the edge and least at the centre.

The polishing should not be proceeded with until the notes on testing have been studied, and during polishing and testing manuscript record should be kept of the observed result of any given mode of working. Reference to such a record at later stages will to some extent compensate for lack of experience.

Means of ascertaining the exact curve possessed by the polished or semi-polished concave glass, must now be considered.

There are many tests, but these instructions will be confined to the Foucault shadow test, which is applied to the unsilvered glass surface in a darkened room.

An artificial star is provided by shading a candle or lamp with an opaque screen punctured with a very tiny hole opposite the brightest part of the flame. The

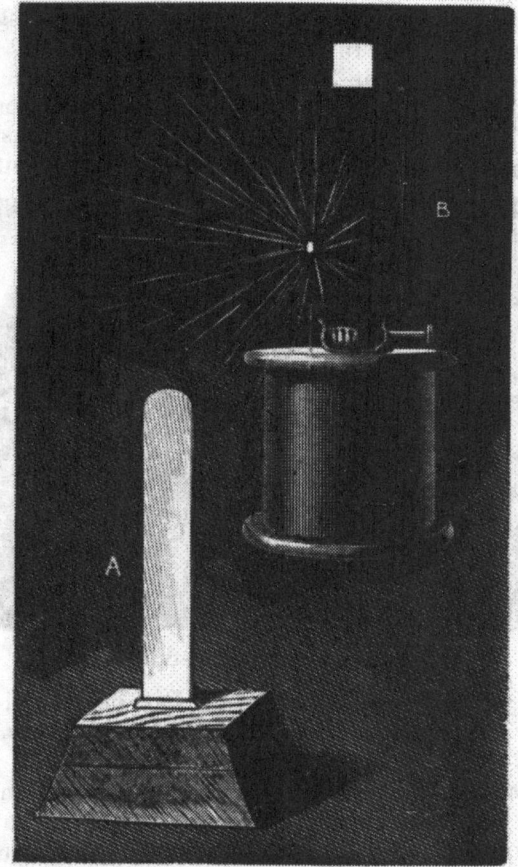

Fig. 281.—Lamp and Blade for Foucault Test.

screen may be conveniently made of a thin metal tube (B, Fig. 281) and the hole may be pierced by a fine needle, after the surface of the metal has been thinned by filing.

132   GLASS WORKING.

The glass being then placed in a darkened room, ten feet (twice the focal length) distant from the lamp, the rays stream out from the hole in the screen and are reflected back and received entirely by the observer's right eye, the glass, though unsilvered, appearing then to be bright, like a full moon.

The observer sits with the lamp close to the right side of his face (see Fig. 282), and brings slowly forward, edgewise, a mounted steel blade (A, Fig. 281), so as to cut right across the cone of reflected rays. The shutter is

Fig. 282.—Foucault Speculum Test.

moved always from left to right. Part of the full-moon mirror surface darkens as the blade shuts away the related rays.

If the shutter is inside the focus, the speculum will appear shaded as in Fig. 283, for the reason indicated in the diagram. If the shutter be outside the focus, the appearance will be as in Fig. 284, where the cause is explained also. If the shutter cut the rays exactly at the focus, the mirror will present an appearance as in Fig. 285—that is, a kind of twilight, regular or irregular, will simultaneously cover the surface, and will as simultaneously fade into blackness as the shutter is moved more forward. This point must be carefully found by experiment. The testing is always performed with the shutter in this position—exactly at the focal point. It is by the character and the intensity of the shadows which appear on the mirror, when the shutter is moved forward across this focus of the reflected rays, that the nature of the mirror curve is determined. With a spherical mirror all the rays are equally affected,

 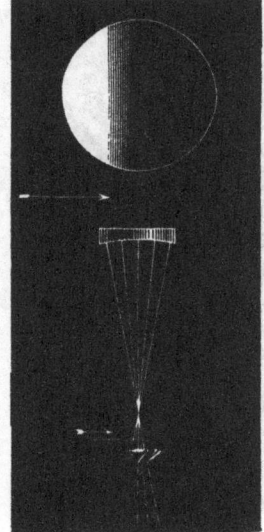

Fig. 283. Fig. 284.

Fig. 283.—Shadow with Shutter inside Focus; Fig. 284.—Shadow with Shutter outside Focus.

and the mirror becomes uniformly grey and black; but in the case of a mirror not spherical, the focus is only approximate, and as the shutter blocks away certain rays and leaves others free to enter the eye, some parts of the mirror surface only are darkened.

The sphere deepens to the ellipse, and the ellipse to the parabola. The oblate (or flattened) sphere comes in order before the sphere, and is a curve which needs to be deepened to make it spherical. The hyperbola lies at the other extreme, and is reached when the spherical curve has been too much modified in the attempt to parabolise.

The shadow-markings read at the centre of curvature fall naturally into three classes, though it requires experience in testing to decide where the distinctive

 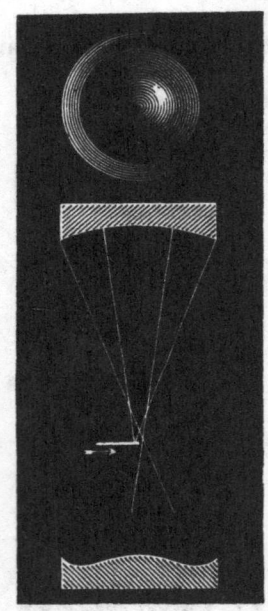

Fig. 285.   Fig. 286

Fig. 285.—Shadow with Shutter at Focus of Special Mirror; Fig. 286.—Oblate Spheroid.

shading of the one class merges into that of the other, so delicate is the test.

The classes are : (a) The oblate spheroid (Fig. 286); (b) the sphere (Fig. 287); (c) the ellipse, parabola, hyperbola (Fig. 288).

In the third division the shadow-markings are identical in each case, the classification depending only upon the intensity of light and shade.

If desired, a section-surface may be projected by

imagining light as streaming obliquely on the mirror from right to left, the direction opposite to that in which the shutter moves. Then the existence of shade will import the existence of a hill to cast the shade, and the degree of intensity of light and shadow will give an indication of the magnitude of the hill. This will be understood by a reference to the diagrams.

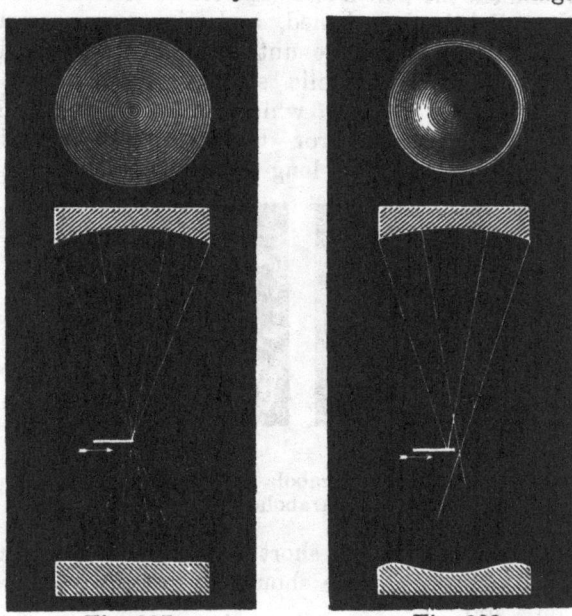

Fig. 287. Fig. 288.
Fig. 287.—Sphere; Fig. 288.—Hyperbola.

In the sphere (Fig. 287), where the shade is diffused and regular, the section given is flat, while in the oblate spheroid (Fig. 286) there is a noticeable elevation at centre and edge; and this order is reversed in the ellipse, parabola, and hyperbola (Fig. 288).

To reduce the oblate spheroid (Fig. 286) to the sphere (Fig. 287) it is necessary to polish away the central hill and the raised edges. These two things can be accomplished by the one process of carefully deepening the mirror from centre to edge, the hill and the edge elevaions disappearing together.

In other words, if the speculum shows, under test, marked shadows of the character of Fig. 286, as is very probable and most desirable, work should be continued with a short, straight stroke, carefully testing at intervals until the polish is complete. Then the stroke may be slightly lengthened, and the curve carried cautiously past the sphere until the faintest possible indication of the parabolic shadow appears (as in Figs. 289 or 290), either of which shadow-figures might be shown by a perfect mirror—the fainter shadow being proper to a speculum of long focus, and the stronger

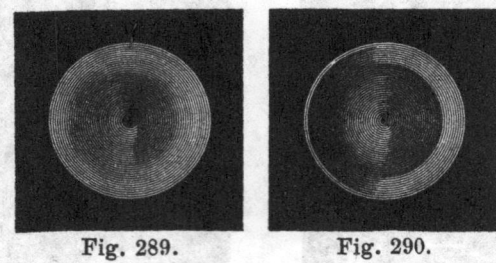

Fig. 289. Fig. 290.

Fig. 289.—Long Focus Parabola; Fig 290.—Short Focus Parabola.

shadow proper to one of short focus. In any case, the speculum at such a stage should be tested, in the testtube, on a star.

If, on the contrary, the shadow, as in Fig. 288, is noticeably marked, or, indeed, appear at all before polish is complete, the curve must be brought back towards the sphere by the use of one-fourth (or less) rigidly straight strokes, so as to wear away the slight elevation between the centre and the edge.

The difficulty of this last task sometimes necessitates a return to the final stage of fine grinding, and for this reason it is desirable to test the mirror directly polish begins to appear, so that the proper stroke may be used from the commencement in the polishing.

To silver a speculum the following materials are necessary :—Potash (pure by alcohol), aqua ammonia, nitric acid, silver nitrate, alcohol (pure), loaf-sugar (pure), distilled (or rain) water.

These are made up into four solutions, in the following proportions :—(*a*) *The Silver Solution:* Silver nitrate, 50 grs. ; distilled water, 2 oz. fluid. (*b*) *The Potash Solution:* Potash (pure by alcohol), 50 grs. ; distilled water, 2 oz. fluid. (*c*) *Ammonia Solution.* (*d*) *The Reducing Solution:* Loaf-sugar, 840 grs. ; nitric acid, 39 grs. ; alcohol (pure), 25 drs. ; distilled water, 300 grs. Mix and make up to 25 oz. fluid with distilled water.

Two glass or earthenware dishes must be provided, each a little larger in diameter than the speculum, and

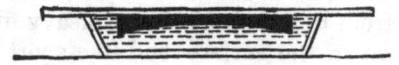

Fig. 291.—Speculum in Silvering Bath.

about 2 in. deep. Cement firmly with pitch a piece of wood to the back of the speculum, so that it may be suspended face downwards within either dish (Fig. 291). The dishes should be thoroughly cleansed.

With nitric acid and a little pad of cotton-wool wash the speculum surface, and then, in one of the dishes, immerse it to a depth of ½ in. in distilled water. Rock the dish slightly. Remove the speculum, and examine the surface. If it be covered with an unbroken film of water it is chemically clean, and may be re-immersed and left till the other bath is prepared.

Put aside in a phial one-tenth part of the silver solution (*a*), and pour the remaining nine-tenths into the second dish. Add ammonia solution drop by drop. A precipitate will form, and disappear as the ammonia is slowly added and stirred in with a glass rod. Then add the potash solution (*b*), Again a precipitate will appear, and again, drop by drop, ammonia must be added to remove it. But, throughout, the less the quantity of ammonia used the more durable will be the silver film.

The bath being clear, take the tenth part of the silver solution that was set aside, and with great care add sufficient to bring the colour of the bath to a warm saffron without causing any precipitate to appear, for the transparency of the bath must not be destroyed. Add distilled water until there is sufficient of the bath to permit the speculum to be immersed to the depth of about ½ in.

Finally, add 4 drs. (fluid) of the reducing solution (*d*), and stir until the colour changes from warm saffron to a pale pink. Then transfer the speculum from the other dish, and lower it into the new bath slantwise, so as to avoid air-bubbles.

The colour will proceed to change from pink to brown, and from brown to black. A heavy film of silver will be thrown to the surface, and in a short time, varying with the temperature, it will be noticed, on moving the surface film with a glass rod, that the bath has become muddy and turbid.

The speculum should then be raised, and will be found to be coated with an unbroken film of pure silver.

This film should be first swilled gently with ordinary water, and then for a time with distilled or rain-water, but thereafter not at all tampered with until it is quite dry, when it may be polished lightly with a little pad of soft chamois leather stuffed with loose cotton-wool and touched with the finest rouge. The polishing should be done with a tiny spiral stroke.

The thickness of the silver thus deposited has been calculated to be not more than one two-hundred-thousandth part of an inch, so that it demands light handling, but it is surprisingly hard, and will last for years with proper care.

The flat will, of course, be silvered by the same process, using solutions made in smaller quantity, but of the same proportional strength. The quantities given are suited for about twenty square inches of surface.

The reducing solution is better if made and kept in stock, but the others will need each time to be freshly prepared.

The silvering is best performed in a warm room, in which all the materials, speculum, water, and dishes, have been left standing sufficiently long to be of the same temperature.

Whilst dealing with the silvering of telescope specula, it may not be out of place to give very brief outlines of four of the better known methods of silvering plate or other sheet glass in the making of mirrors.

One method of silvering glass is to dissolve 30 gr. of nitrate of silver in 3 oz. of distilled water, and, whilst stirring, add strong liquor ammonia till the brown precipitate is re-dissolved. Dissolve 10 gr. of pure Rochelle salts in 1 oz. of distilled water, and mix with the other solution. The sheet of glass should previously be well cleaned and polished, and warmed until a temperature of about 70° or 80° F. is reached. The mixture should then be poured upon the surface of the glass, when silver will be deposited.

Another method is to take a sheet of tinfoil cut so that it measures a little larger every way than the glass to be silvered. The glass is cleaned as before, mercury poured upon it, and the smooth foil laid on, care being taken that no air bubbles form between the foil and the glass. A level surface is then placed upon the foil and weighted for some hours, till mercury ceases to be squeezed out.

A third method is to mix together 1 oz. of coarsely pulverised nitrate of silver, $\frac{1}{2}$ oz. of spirit of hartshorn, and 2 oz. of water, and, after the mixture has stood for twenty-four hours, to pass it through a filter. To the deposit on the filter paper must be added 3 oz. of methylated spirit at 60° over proof and thirty drops of oil of cassia. This should stand untouched for six or eight hours, when a mixture of one part by measure of oil of cloves and two parts of spirit of wine should be added to it. The whole should then immediately be poured upon the glass, which should have a wall of wax or putty around its edges, and allowed to remain for two or three hours.

By the fourth method the glass is well washed, and, whilst it is still wet, a solution of gelatine or other mordant is poured over it. Before the mordant dries, cover the glass with a saturated solution of nitrate of silver, and allow to remain untouched for ten minutes. Wipe with a leather squeegee and give a second application of the nitrate solution. These latter operations should take place with the glass laid upon a slate slab, under which is a trough holding hot water. A final wiping with the squeegee completes the process.

It may be mentioned that glass is gilt only by laying upon it gold leaf as described on p. 96; there is no practicable method of gilding glass by the precipitation of any metal dissolved or suspended in a liquid as in the silvering processes noted above.

CHAPTER VIII.

TURNING, CHIPPING, AND GRINDING GLASS.

ALTHOUGH the processes of turning metal and glass resemble each other in some particulars, yet there are many points of difference. Metals are turned in the lathe at a speed suited to their nature; and, whatever the tool used, the speed has a great deal to do with its efficiency. Now, with glass, the nature of the cutting-tool is an important matter. One tool will only require a speed as slow as that used for turning steel, whilst another will want a speed equal to that required for a polishing bob. Another difference is that an oil-stone is always in requisition for the cutting-edge of metal-turning tools, but the rough edge left from the grindstone gives the best results for glass.

In knocking a metal casting into a wood chuck, or bolting a piece of work to a face-plate, a hammer has to be used to set the casting true, or the spanner is used for a tap here and there for trueing it on the face-plate; but with a piece of glass there are no boxwood chucks, no face-plates, no tapping true with spanner or hammer, as a slight knock would shatter or splinter he brittle glass. Some information on this part of the subject has been given in the preceding chapter.

Before glass is ready for the emery smoothing process, it has to be got near to the required curve. The piece of soft flint glass is first faceted—that is, small windows are ground and polished—so as to enable the workman to examine the interior of the glass for feathers, specks, veins, air-bubbles, and dead metal, for any of the above would spoil the lens. If the piece of glass is square and free from imperfections, it is "shanked" to nearly the size required for working. The softer the iron of which the "shanks," Fig. 296, p. 148, are made, the better will be the result, for they are required to bite the edge of the glass. With a slight turn of the wrist a splinter of glass is taken off the edge, in some cases exactly perpendicular, but more generally with a tendency to a bead-shape. Shanks made of steel do not bite; they slip, and only result in flawing.

The piece of glass being near the size required, it

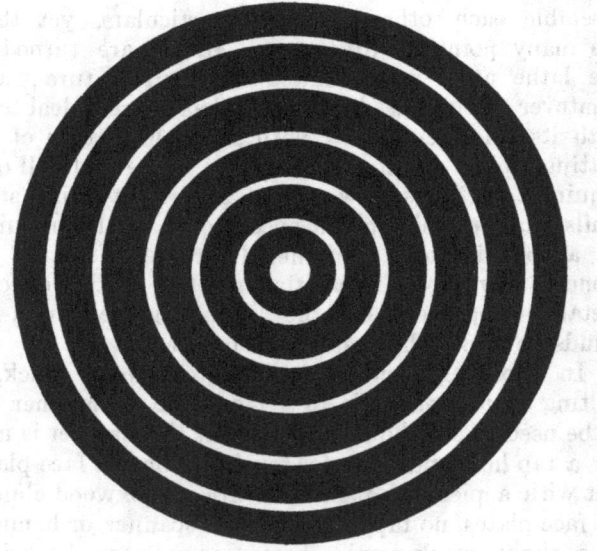

Fig. 292.—Chuck for Holding Glass.

must be chucked in the lathe. Now, it cannot be put in a wood chuck, for it is not to be knocked; it cannot be put on a face-plate, for the pressure of a bolt would break it; so it must be fixed to a chuck by a medium which will hold it. If it were stuck on a flat chuck, the expansion or shrinkage of the metal caused by the differences in the temperature would start the lens, pulling pieces out of the glass. To prevent this, formerly a layer of pitch was placed between the glass and the metal chuck.

TURNING, CHIPPING, AND GRINDING GLASS. 143

It has been found that a pewter chuck is best when turning the first surfaces of lenses. This runner, as it is called, is made partly of brass screwed on the nose of the lathe; then a layer of pewter is cast on, which is turned to the sizes required, and a number of recesses cut in it so that not much of the metal is in actual contact with the glass. These recesses are filled up with

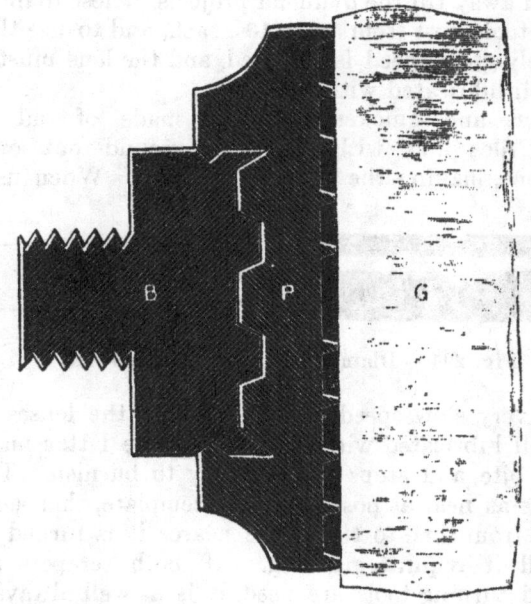

Fig. 293.—Section of Chuck.

a composition of oil of cloves and shellac. The glass is warmed and laid on the chuck, and set true.

Fig. 292 shows the face of the chuck; the black lines show the wax composition, and the white lines the pewter. Fig. 293 is a section showing the brass chuck, B, the layer of pewter, P, and the glass, G, cemented to it. The chuck is screwed on the lathe, and the piece of glass is now ready to be turned, the T-rest being placed so that it just clears the rough edge.

As to the turning-tools, the expensive ones consist of faulty diamonds mounted at the end of a piece of steel, so that the rough edge projects from the top. The method of mounting them is shown in Fig. 294. A piece of steel is drilled down $\frac{1}{10}$th of an inch, the diamond placed in the hole, and the end knocked over with a hammer; the hole is then silver-soldered up, and the end filed away till the diamond projects. These diamond turning-tools cost from 5s. to 10s. each, and to use them effectively great speed is required, and the lens must be kept well lubricated with water.

Other, and quicker, tools are made of old triangular files and with the teeth ground out on a grindstone, making the edges very sharp. When using

Fig. 294.—Diamond Point Turning-tools.

these a very slow speed is required, and the lenses are kept well lubricated with turpentine; the latter makes the file bite, and stops its tendency to burnish. Turn the glass as near as possible to the template, sharpening the files from time to time; the nearer it is turned the less will it require grinding. If both scrapers and diamond turning-tools are used, it is as well always to finish with the diamonds, as a somewhat smoother surface can be obtained by their use. The time it will take to turn the glass to the curve depends on its nature, some being almost as soft as wood to turn, and other kinds as hard as pebble.

Fig. 295 shows a double convex lens as it would be left by the turner ready for smoothing, and the style of the chuck used. Lenses may be shaped much more quickly by turning than by grinding.

As a contrast to the above method of shaping glass, the system of making photographic and other lenses as adopted at a large and well-known factory may be considered.

Each block of glass, which must be of the finest quality, has its physical properties tested before being worked, a small sample prism being made from the block for the purpose. The exact curves of the lens surfaces have then to be calculated. The glass blocks are first roughly shaped and then cut by means of zinc discs

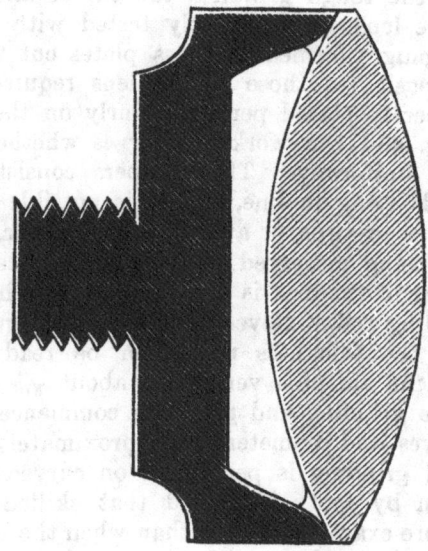

Fig. 295.—Lens in Lathe Chuck.

fed with diamond dust, the edges of the blocks being rounded with glass shears, so giving a cylindrical shape to the cut pieces, which are a little higher and larger in diameter than the required lens. The glass cylinder is then reduced to proper thickness on rotating flat cast-iron discs fed with wet sand, whilst the edge is shaped upon a suitably curved grinder. To rough grind the flat faces to the curves, the worker holds the glass firmly upon a quickly rotating cup-shaped grinder, kept well supplied with wet sand. The grinders are, of course, made convex or concave, according to the form of lens required. In making these grinders, a special lathe with a spherical rest is used and the grinders have to be shaped very carefully, as upon their truth depends the exactness of the lens. The grinders are apt to wear unevenly, and when this occurs they are at once withdrawn and corrected upon the lathe.

During the rough grinding, the curves and dimensions of the lens are frequently tested with callipers and with gauges formed of brass plates cut to curves exactly opposite to those of the lens required. The gauge is merely placed perpendicularly on the surface of the lens, and the worker observes whether it sits everywhere uniformly. The callipers consist of two pointed rods lying in line, and it is possible to slide one of them towards or away from the other, the displacement being measured on an attached scale. The thickest part of the lens is brought between the points, and the sliding rod is moved until the points just touch the glass; the thickness may then be read off the scale with the aid of a vernier to about $\frac{1}{5000}$ in.

The fine grinding and polishing commence as soon as the curves and diameter are approximately correct. The second grinding is performed on curved grinders each driven by foot; it is said that skilled workers produce more exact work thus than when the lathes are power-driven. So that the lenses may be more easily manipulated, each is cemented to a handle, and in the case of small lenses, three or four being attached to the same handle. Fine clean, levigated emery is fed on to the grinding tool, and is mixed with water into a paste; five grades of emery are used, each successive one being finer than the former, the emery being obtained in these various grades by the method explained on pp. 120 and 121. The last and finest grade is levigated for sixty minutes.

During the fine grinding, blocks of glass ground out to curves exactly opposite to those of the required lens are used to test the lenses. A spherometer is also used to measure the curvature. This instrument has a three-legged frame that stands upon three steel pins; in the centre is a vertical and fine thread screw, and by means of a large graduated head this is turned down until its point touches the surface on which the spherometer stands. The degree of sphericity of the surface is shown by the scale alongside the graduated head of the screw; on a plane surface the index points to zero. By bringing the lens and the test glass just mentioned into close contact, any curves which are not uniform are denoted by the colour, position, or irregularity of the Newton colour rings. In this method of testing advantage is taken of the known wave lengths of light, some of which are only ·000003 in. A variation of such a small amount as this can at once be detected. When the lens has assumed its proper form, it is polished to transparency with rouge on the fine grinding tool previously mentioned.

Information on fitting lenses into spectacle frames may hardly be within the scope of a handbook on glass working, but such instruction is given on account of the frequency with which a glass worker is called upon to undertake these jobs.

The tools required for putting a new lens into a spectacle-frame are very few. They include a grindstone; a small screwdriver, or the blade of a small penknife; a pair of shanks, or a pair of goffering-irons, the handle parts of which can be used instead of shanks; or, if nothing else of the same kind is handy, a pair of pliers can be used, though these, being hard, do not bite so well as the soft iron, and are rather liable to splinter the glass by slipping.

Before obtaining the new glass, the necessary focus must be found. When a lens gets broken it is not generally pulverised, so there can generally be found a piece large enough to try its focus; or, if the lenses are of equal foci, the opposite eyeglass can be used for that purpose. For example, suppose the lens broken is convex or positive focus, the best time to try it would be by lamplight. Pin a sheet of white paper on the wall, and put a lamp about 15 ft. away from it; next hold the lens, or the piece of it, between the lamp and the paper, and gradually put the lens closer and closer to the paper till it projects upon the paper a perfectly sharp image of the lamp. Now the distance between the glass and the paper should be measured, and that will be the focus or number of the lens. If this is 18 in., obtain a lens of 18-in. focus; or if 36 in., a No. 36. The lenses cost wholesale from 12s. to 15s. per gross of all numbers,

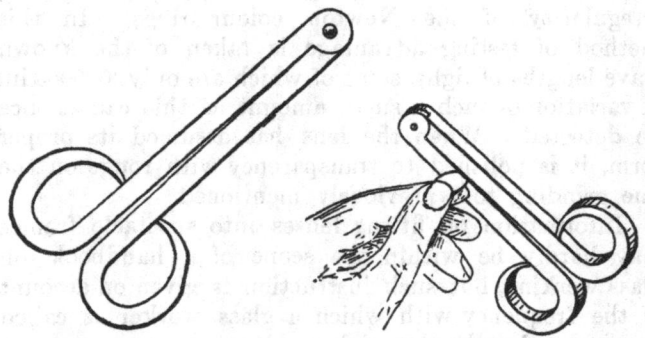

Fig. 296.—Shanks for Nibbling Lenses.

Fig. 297.—Nibbling Lens with Shanks.

from 6-in. to 70-in. focus, but the deeper ones, from 6-in. to 1-in., are more costly; pebbles cost from 16s. to 25s. per dozen. A single pair of lenses will cost 4d., an odd lens 3d. Having got the lens, it will be found to be much larger than the eye of the frame, and to grind this down would take a long time; so it is usual to nibble the edge round till it is got to the same size as the frame in which it is to fit. This can be done with the pair of shanks (Fig. 296), or with the pair of goffering-irons, if these are used instead. During this nibbling hold the lens (as shown in Fig. 297) with the left hand, and with a slight turn of the shanks continually break small pieces from the edge till the proper size is obtained. Of course, the

TURNING, CHIPPING, AND GRINDING GLASS. 149

frame of the spectacles must be referred to for size whilst shanking. Take out the screw, putting it and the arm carefully on one side. Now hold the lens to the grindstone revolving away from the worker (Fig. 298),

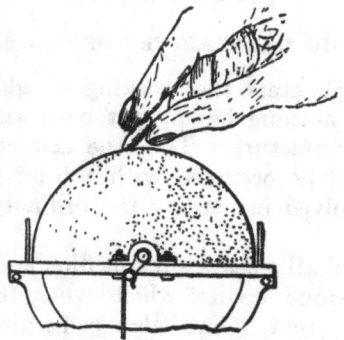

Fig. 298.—Grinding Spectacle Lens.

gradually turning the lens round till a chamfer has been put on one side reaching to the centre of the edge; after that has been done, reverse the glass and put a chamfer on the other side, when the edge should appear as in A Fig. 299. Continue to try the lens in its frame till it is

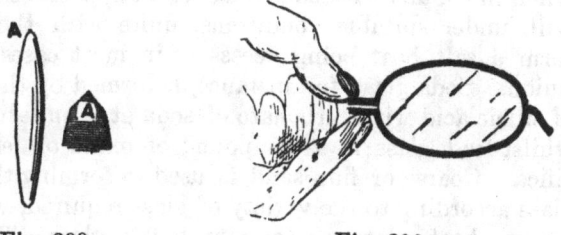

Fig. 299. Fig. 300.
Fig. 299.—Edge of Lens after Grinding. Fig. 300.—Spectacle Lens in Frame.

only a trifle too large, so that there is a slight space between the lugs, as shown in Fig. 300; these can be drawn together with the screw thus holding the lens perfectly tight.

CHAPTER IX.

THE MANUFACTURE OF GLASS.

IN previous chapters the working of glass has alone been treated, nothing having yet been said concerning its actual manufacture. This, the last chapter, therefore, may well be occupied with a brief *résumé* of the processes involved in making the ordinary varieties of glass.

The basis of all glass is silex or flint and alkali, these being two opaque bodies which when fused together become transparent. The silex is furnished by sand, whose principal constituent is silica. Alkalies commonly used in making glass are salts of soda or potash and lime ; sometimes oxide of lead (litharge) takes the place of the lime, and instead of the salts mentioned, barilla, kelp, or wood-ash may be used for inferior glass, the impurities contained by these substances even helping to fuse the silica. Silica is the oxide of silicon, and when in contact with substances of an opposite character will, under suitable conditions, unite with them and form a salt, heat being necessary in most cases to the union. Soda glass, for instance, is formed by the union of silicic acid with carbonate of soda at a suitable heat, whilst lead glass is a compound of oxide of lead and silica. Coarse or fine sand is used in forming the soda glass according to the variety of glass required, whether crown, sheet, plate, or common bottle glass. The lead glass, known as flint glass, is shaped into the finer works of the glass-blower, being used in the manufacture of superior table glasses, decanters, etc., and imitation gems. It possesses greater transparency and is more brilliant than is the soda glass. Flint glass has a very important use in lens-making ; lead enters into the composition of all optical glass.

THE MANUFACTURE OF GLASS.

The sand used in England for glass-making comes chiefly from Alum Bay in the Isle of Wight; it is important that the sand should contain as few impurities as possible. The most common impurity is oxide of iron, and as this gives a green tinge to the glass its effects have to be counteracted by the addition of black oxide of manganese. The oxide is converted to a peroxide, which imparts a slight yellow hue, though if the manganese oxide be in excess, a purple colour is produced. Arsenic is considered by some to neutralise much more effectually the presence of the oxide of iron than does the black oxide of manganese, and to be more easily managed.

Of course, different makers use different proportions of the ingredients of glass, but the following formulæ may be considered typical of most glass compositions:—

Bohemian Crown Glass:—Sand, 63 parts; potash, 22 parts; lime, 12 parts; manganese oxide, 1 part.

Flint Window Glass:—Sand, 3 parts; red lead, from 2 to 2·5 parts; carbonate of potash, from 1·5 to 1·66 parts; a little saltpetre as an oxidising agent.

Superior Flint Glasses:—(a) Burnt sand, 12 parts; carbonate of potash, 4 parts; oxide of lead, 8 parts; nitrate of potash, from 0·5 to 1 part; oxide of manganese, from 0·0089 to 0·0267 part; sufficient pure flint cullet. (b) Sand, 67 parts; pearlash, 23 parts; powdered slaked lime, 10 parts; manganese 0·25 part; red lead, from 5 to 8 parts. (c) White sand, 15 parts; red lead, 10 parts; wood ash, 4 parts; saltpetre, 1 part; very small quantity each of arsenious acid and manganese oxide.

Green Bottle Glass:—Sand, 10 parts; kelp, 3 to 4 parts; lixiviated wood ashes, from 16 to 17 parts; fresh wood ashes, from 3 to 4 parts; potter's clay, from 8 to 10 parts; cullet or broken glass, 10 parts.

Optical Glasses:—(a) Silica, 10 parts; oxide of lead, 10 parts; potash, 2·3 parts; borax, 0·07 part. (b) Silica, 10 parts; oxide of lead, 10 parts; potash, 2·3 parts; saltpetre, 0·13 part; borax, 0·18 part.

Peligot's Bohemian Tube Glass:—Silica, 71·5 parts; dry carbonate of potassa, 20 parts; quicklime, 8½ parts; a little manganese; very small quantity of borax or boracic acid to assist fusion.

Plate Glasses:—(a) Sand, 4 parts; dry carbonate of soda, 26·5 parts; lime, 4 parts; saltpetre, 1·5 parts; broken glass of same kind, 25 parts. (b) Sand, 10 parts; calcined soda sulphate, 5 parts; lime, 2 parts; charcoal, 0·275 part. (c) White sand, 30 parts; broken glass of same kind, 30 parts; dry soda carbonate, 10 parts; slaked lime, 4·3 parts. (d) Sand, 7·2 parts; refined soda, 4·5 parts; quicklime, 4·8 parts; nitre, 0·25 part; broken glass of same kind, 4·5 parts.

Pompeian Glass:—Sand, 4 parts; soda, 1 part; lime, 0·5 part; a small quantity of alumina.

Soda Crystal Glasses:—(a) Potashes, 6 parts; sand, 12 parts; chalk, 2·4 parts; saltpetre, 0·2 part; arsenious acid, 0·2 part; oxide of manganese, 0·006 part. (b) Pearlash, 7 parts; white sand, 12 parts; saltpetre, 1 part; arsenious acid, 0·05 part; manganese oxide, ·03 part.

Soda Window Glass:—Sand, 4 parts; sulphate of soda, 2 parts; lime, from ·8 to 1 part; a small quantity of charcoal.

White Table Glasses:—(a) Potashes, 40 parts; chalk, 11 parts; sand, 76 parts; manganese oxide, 0·5 part; white cullet, 95 parts. (b) Potashes, 25 parts; sand, 50 parts; chalk, 10 parts; saltpetre, 1 part. (c) Potashes, 20 parts; dry Glauber salts, 11 parts; soaper salt, 16 parts; sand, 55 parts; cullet or broken glass of same kind, 140 parts. (d) Sand, 10 parts; kelp, 23·5 parts; wood ashes, 6 parts; broken glass of same kind, 10 parts; manganese oxide, 0·133 part.

White Window Glass:—Sand, 50 parts; dry sulphate of soda, 25 parts; powdered quicklime, from 8·5 to 10 parts; charcoal, 2 parts.

In the actual making of the glass the ingredients are first thoroughly mixed, and it is the custom in some foundries partially to heat the mixture, which is then known as frit. This preliminary heating is in some cases dispensed with. The frit or the raw mixture, as the case may be, is then put into glass-pots, previously placed in the furnace. These glass-pots are made of fireclay, and for window glass are uncovered, the fire passing over them; for flint glass the pots are covered, an opening being left in front for the convenience of the blower. Any scum that may rise to the surface of the glass in process of making is removed with iron ladles.

A continuously high temperature is necessary for the perfect fusion and amalgamation of the ingredients, and for the expulsion of impurities. These latter processes are greatly helped by throwing in at intervals small quantities of broken glass of precisely the same kind as is being made. When all impurities have been discharged and skimmed off, the molten glass, which in this condition is known as metal, appears colourless and translucent and the vitrification is complete. The temperature of the furnace is then lowered until the glass is less of a fluid and more of a paste, sufficiently consistent to be tenacious but yet soft enough to be shaped without risk of cracking. The vitrification usually occupies from forty-eight to seventy-two hours.

Glass is coloured in the molten state by admixture with metallic oxides. Reds, greens, and blues are imparted by copper oxides; cobalt also produces blue. A fine pink is given by oxide of gold; an increased quantity of the latter produces a red colour. For green or yellow, oxide of iron may be used. Purple and black are produced by black oxide of manganese. Yellows of various depths are produced by oxide of silver, which, however, is not melted in the glass-pot with the other ingredients. The silver oxide is mixed with chalk or similar substance and laid on the cold glass, which is then heated to a dull red; the quantity of oxide used determines the strength of the tint. Red produced by oxide of gold and copper red are coated over clear glass, which is afterwards heated.

In making sheet glass, the end of a 5-ft. or 6-ft. iron blow-tube is dipped into a glass-pot, and by a twisting motion a lump of doughy metal (soft glass) is gathered at the end of it. On the upper end of the blow-tube is a mouth-piece, and there is a smaller opening at the lower conical end, this opening getting wider towards the middle of the tube. The lump of soft glass is then blown into a pear shape, and rolled on a smooth marble or iron slab, called a marver, afterwards being swung from side to side over a pit until it is drawn out to a true cylinder having a length of fifty or sixty inches. It is then again heated in the furnace, the cool end of the iron tube is closed with the finger, and the hot expanding air within the glass cylinder bursts the heated end, which is then reduced whilst hot with an iron tool to the diameter of the rest of the cylinder. By drawing a thread of hot glass round the shoulder of the cylinder and making a crack by applying a cold iron, the cylinder is easily detached from the blow-tube; it is then scratched lengthwise internally with a diamond and placed in a flattening kiln, being opened out when soft with wooden tools where the line has been scored by the diamond. The glass, under the influence of the heat, then flattens out on the smooth floor of the kiln. When this glass is polished, it forms an inferior kind of plate glass.

Curved sheet glass is formed by substituting for the flat floor of the kiln smooth blocks of iron having surfaces curved to the required shape of the glass. The glass to be bent is placed upon the curved blocks in the furnace whilst the latter is cold.

Commoner crown glass is made by opening the globe directly it is blown, re-heating it, and trundling it round until the heated sides start suddenly into a disc, having a thick bull's-eye in the middle. This glass and that produced by the method previously noted are annealed and cut up for window glass. It may here be mentioned that all glass, after having been shaped, is annealed by raising it to a certain temperature in, say, a muffle and then allowing it to cool slowly. The particles of the glass, after it leaves the furnace and after it is shaped, take a long time to arrange themselves; if the glass is not annealed, it is very brittle, and when suddenly heated is liable to crack as a result of unequal expansion. Annealing renders the glass less liable to crack, but if the temperature of the annealing furnace is too high or is maintained for too long a time, the glass loses its transparency and assumes a crystalline texture. This loss of transparency is known as devitrification.

The formation of an inferior plate glass by opening out blown glass cylinders has already been mentioned, but good plate glass is not produced by blowing, but in the following manner. When the materials have been properly fused and vitrified (that is, rendered transparent) in the furnace, the glass is transferred from the melting pot to a large vessel known as a cuvette, which is placed for some hours in the furnace. When withdrawn it is raised and suspended by a crane, the glass flowing out on to a table which has edges raised to suit the thickness of the glass. An iron roller distributes the glass over the table, and when cold the plate is placed on the floor of an annealing oven; the latter is sealed up, and the plate glass left to cool, two weeks being generally allowed for this.

On withdrawal from the annealing oven, two plates may be brought into contact with each other and their surfaces ground with sand or similar abrasive material and water. A glass plate is firmly fixed with plaster-of-Paris on the top of the grinding bench, and another plate is fixed on the underside of a heavy travelling table, which moves with a rotatory and oscillating motion. The abrasive material is fed in, and thus one plate grinds the other. This grinding is succeeded by a series of hand-grindings, emery powder of gradually increasing fineness being used to remove the marks caused by the machine grinding.

Plate glass is polished with a woollen cushion on

which is a little hydrated oxide of iron. The cushion is attached to a handle which is machine-driven, hand labour failing to produce a good polish so regularly and systematically.

In blowing, say, a bottle, the iron blow-tube is dipped into the glass pot and twisted round so as to take up a mass of the soft glass. A hollow ball is then blown, which is shaped with a shear-like instrument as it is rotated on the glass-maker's chair. The glass is broken off the blow-tube, re-heated, and the mouth of the bottle is formed. Any coloured or other glass to be added is then heated and stuck on whilst the bottle is being rotated; the coloured glass may be shaped, if desired, with a hand-stamp or die. During these processes, the bottle may require to be re-heated several times.

A method adopted in forming cheap glass bottles is to blow out some glass at the end of a blow-tube and then impart the desired shape in forms or moulds situated in the floor and closed by means of a foot-lever. On removal from the mould the bottle is broken off the tube, re-heated, and the mouth formed as before.

INDEX.

Absorption Tubes, 60
Acid for Etching Glass, 93
—— Vats, 88
Adapters, Making, 101
Air-pumps, Water, 73
Air Traps of Barometers, 67
Alkalies for making Glass, 150
Annealing Glass, 154, 155
Arm-rest used in Etching Glass, 91

Barometer Air Traps, 67
—— Bulbs, Forming, 62
—— Float, Making, 39
—— Tube, 32
Batswing Flame, Bending Tubes in, 29
Beaker, Re-making Mouth of, 100
——, Making Cover-glass from, 100
Beeswax, 26
Bellows, 18, 19
—— fitted to Bench, 18
Bending Glass Tubes, 29, 30–32
Black Glass, 153
Black's Mouth Blowpipe, 10
Blowers, 13, 14, 18, 19
Blowing Glass Articles (see Glass Blowing and under separate headings, Bulbs, Funnels, etc.)
Blowpipe, Black's, 10
—— Flame, Bending Tubes in, 29
—— Flames, 27, 28
——, Foot, 9
——, Mouth, 9–12
——, Spirit, 10–12
Blow-tube, Glass-worker's, 154
Blue Glass, 153
Bohemian Crown Glass, 151
—— Tube Glass, Peligot's, 152
Boring Holes in Glass, 103–112
Bottle Glass, Green, 151
Bottles, Blowing, 156
——, Cutting (see Tubing)
——, Gutta-percha, 87
——, Broken, Utilising, 102, 103
Brass Tube Drill for Glass, 107
Broken Apparatus, Mending and Utilising, 97–103
Bronze Tube Drill for Glass, 105
Bulb, Barometer, Blowing, 62
——, Forming, on Centre of Tube, 57, 58
—— penetrated by Tubes, 67–71
—— Pipettes, Forming, 55, 56
—— Tubes, 49

Bulb, Sealing Platinum Wires within, 73–75
——, Thermometer, Blowing, 62
Bulbs, Blowing, 49–64
——, Electric Lamp, 62
——, ——, ——, Sealing Wires within, 73–75
——, Joining Tubes to, 65
——, Liebig's Potash, 60
——, Oval, Blowing, 60–62
——, Several, Formed on one Tube, 59, 60
Bunsen Burners, 20–23

Callipers for Testing Lenses, 146
Cements for Glass, 112
Charcoal Cones for forming Lips on Tubes, 26, 40
China, Riveting, 107–112
Chucking Glass in Lathe, 142, 143
Cigarette-holder, Blowing, 84–86
Coloured Glass, Ornamenting blown goods with, 81, 85,
—— Glasses, 153
Colouring Glass, 153
Concave Curve Gauge, 119
Convex Curve Gauge, 119
—— Tool used in Speculum working, 114
Copper Drill-bits, 108
—— Tool for forming Lips on Tubes, 26, 40
—— Tube-drill for Glass, 105
Cover-glass made from Beaker, 100
Crown Glass, Making, 154
—— ——, Recipes for, 151
Curve Gauge for Specula, 116, 119

Deflagrating Jar, Making, 103
Diamond Drill for Glass, 108
—— Point Turning Tools, 144 ¹
—— Sparks for Drilling Glass, 108
Dipping Vat, Steam, 87, 88
Dishes, Making, from Cracked Apparatus, 100, 101
Distillation Flask, Fractional, 63, 64
Drainer, 87
Draper's Table of Emery Grades, 121
Drawing down Glass Tubing, 54
Drill, Diamond, for Glass, 108
Drill-bits or Drill-tubes, 108
Drilling Holes in Glass, 103–112
—— —— —— ——, Lubrication used for, 104, 106

Drills for Glass, 103, 104, 105, 107, 108
Dropping Rods, 39

Electric Lamp Bulbs, 62, 73-75
Embossing Glass, 95, 96
Emery Grades, Draper's Table of, 121
——, Ross's Table of, 121
——, Separation of, into Grades, 120 121
—— for Glass Drilling, 105, 107
—— —— Speculum working, 120-122
Etching Glass, Acid for, 92
—— —— Fancy Articles, 87-95
——, Resist for, 89, 92
Eudiometer, Making, 73

Faceted Speculum Polisher, 126
Faceting Glass for Lens Making, 141
—— Tool, 126
Fancy Glass Articles, Blowing, 81-86
—— —— ——, Etching, 87-95
File for Cutting Tubes, 26
——, Using, as Drill for Glass, 106
Filter Pumps, Making, 69-73
Finkener's Water Air.pump, 73
Flame, Batswing, Bending Tubes in, 29
——, Blowpipe, Bending Tubes in, 30-32
——, Large Blowpipe, 27
——, Small Blowpipe, 27
——, Smoky, 28
——, Spirit Lamp, Bending Tubes in, 32
Flasks, Blowing, 49-64
—— Cracked, Re-making Necks of, 100
——, Fractional Distillation, 63, 64
——, Large, Blowing, 52-54
——, Making Dishes from, 100
——, Pasteur's, 64
——, Small, Blowing, 49-52
—— with Side Tubes, 63, 64
Flint Glass, 150, 151
—— ——, Glass-pots for, 153
—— ——, Tubes of, 26
Focal Length of Spectacle Lens, Ascertaining, 147
—— —— —— Speculum, Testing, 125
Foot Bellows, 18, 19
—— Blowpipe, 9
Foucault Shadow Test for Speculum, 130-136
Fractional Distillation Flasks, 63, 64
Frit, Glass, 153
Funnel, Forming, 79, 80
Funnels, Separatory, 80
—— with Stopcocks, 80
——, Thistle, Making, 75-78, 102

Gallenkamp's Vacuum Tubes, 85
Gas Blowpipe, 16
—— Jet, Bending Tubes in, 29
Gauges for Testing Lenses, 146
—— —— —— Specula, 116, 119
Gilding Glass, 95, 96

Gilding Glass by Precipitation, 140
Glass, Alkalies for Making, 150
——, Annealing, 154, 155
—— Apparatus, Broken, Utilising, 97-103
——, Black, 153
—— Blowing (see Bulbs, Flasks, Funnels, etc.)
—— ——, Beeswax for, 26
—— ——, Charcoal Cones for, 26
—— ——, Copper Tool for, 26
—— ——, Heating Appliances used in, 9-25
—— ——, Materials for, 26
—— —— on Large Scale, 35, 48
—— ——, Triangular Tool for, 26
——, Blue, 153
——, Bohemian, Recipes for, 151, 152
——, Boring Holes in, 103-112
——, Cements for, 112
——, Colouring, 153
——, Crown, Making, 154
——, Curved Sheet, Making, 154
——, Embossing, 96, 97
——, Flint, 150, 151
——, ——, Glass-pots for, 153
——, ——, Tubes of, 26
—— Frit, 153
——, Gilding and Embossing, 96, 97
——, ——, by Precipitation, 140
——, Green, 151, 153
——, Ingredients of, 150-152
——, Lead (See Glass, Flint)
——, Litharge used in making, 150
——, Manufacture of, 150-156
——, Methods of Working, 9-
——, Molten, or "Metal," 153
——, Optical, Recipes for, 151
——, Oxide of Lead for making, 150
——, Peligot's Bohemian Tube, 152
——, Pink, 153
—— Pipes, Blowing, 81-84
——, Plate, Grinding, 155
——, ——, Making, 152, 154, 155
——, ——, Polishing, 155, 156
——, Pompeian, Recipes for, 152
——, Purple, 153
——, Red, 153
—— Riveting, 107-112
—— Rod, Working, 38, 39
—— Rods for Dropping Purposes, 39
——, Sand used in making, 150, 151
——, Sheet, Gilding and Embossing, 96, 97
——, ——, Making, 154
——, ——, Silvering, 139, 140
——, Silica for making, 150
——, Silex for making, 150
——, Silvering, 137-140
——, Soda, 150, 152
——, Turning, in Lathe, 141-144
——, Yellow, 153
——, White, Recipes for, 152
Glasses, Test, Making, 79

INDEX.

Glasses, Wine, Etching, 87–95
——, ——, Making, 78, 79
Glass-pots, 153
Glow-lamp, Making, 62, 73–75
Green Glass, 151, 153
Grinding Plate Glass, 155
Grindstone, Rubbing down Edge of Lens on, 149
——, —— —— —— —— Speculum on, 117
Gutta-percha Bottle, 87

Hardening Drills for Glass, 104, 105
Heating Appliances used in Glass Blowing, 9–25
Holes, Boring, in Glass, 103–112
Hone Squares Tool used in Speculum Working, 114

Incandescent Electric Lamp Bulbs, Making, 62, 73–75

Jar, Deflagrating, Making 103
——, Making, from Broken Bottle, 102
Joining Tubes, 40–48

Ladle, 87
Lamps, Spirit, 23–25
Lathe, Chucking Glass in, 142, 143
——, Tools for Turning Glass in, 144
——, Working Glass in, 117, 141–144
Lead Glass (see Flint Glass)
—— Oxide used in Glass Making, 15
Lens, Callipers for Testing, 146
——, Flint Glass for making, 151
——, Gauge for Testing, 146
—— Making, Faceting Glass for, 141
—— —— in the Lathe, 141–144
—— —— on the Continent, 145–147
——, Newton Test for, 147
——, Photographic, Making, 145–147
——, Spectacle, Ascertaining Focus of, 147
——, ——, Fitting, 147–149
——, ——, Grinding Edges of, 149
——, ——, Shanks for Nibbling, 148, 149
——, Spherometer for measuring Curvature of, 147
Liebig's Potash Bulbs, 60
Litharge used in Glass Making, 150

Marver, 154
"Metal" or Molten Glass, 153
Mirror Making, 139, 140
Mouth Blowpipe, 9–12

Newton Colour Ring Test, 147
Nippers for Wire Rivet making, 111

Optical Glasses, Recipes for, 151
Oval Bulbs, Blowing, 60–62
Oxide of Lead used in Making Glass, 150

Pasteur's Flasks, 64
Peligot's Bohemian Tube Glass, 152
Pencil Sticks, 87, 91
Pewter Lathe-chucks for holding Glass, 143
Photographic Lenses, Making, 145–147
Pin, Pouncing, 87
Pink Glass, 153
Pipette, Broken, Making Thistle Funnel from, 102
——, Bulb, Forming, 55, 56
Pipettes, Forming, 55, 56, 102
Pitch Pads for Polishing Specula, 126, 128
—— used in Speculum Working, 122, 126, 128
Plate Glass, Grinding, 155
—— ——, Making, 154, 155
—— ——, Polishing, 155, 156
—— ——, Recipes for, 152
Plates, Glass or China, Riveting, 107–112
Platinum Wires, Sealing, within Bulb, 73–75
Polishing Specula, 125–130
Pompeian Glass, Recipe for, 152
Potash Bulbs, Liebig's, 60
Pounce used in Etching Glass, 90
Pouncing Pin, 87
Pumps, Filter, Making, 69–73
——, Water Air, 73
Purple Glass, 153

Red Glass, 153
Resist used in Etching Glass, 89, 92
Retort, Making Adapters from, 101;
——, —— Dishes from, 101
——, Re-making, 101
Riveting Glass, 107–112
Rod, Glass, Working, 38, 39
Rods, Dropping, Making, 39
Rosse Machine, Tracing from, 123
Ross's Table of Emery Grades, 121
Rouge for Speculum Polishing, 122, 128

Sand used in Glass Making, 150, 151
—— —— —— Speculum Working, 120
Sealing Tubes, 84–88
Shadow Test, Foucault, for Speculum, 130, 136
Shanks for Nibbling Glass, 142, 148, 149
Sheet Glass, 154
—— ——, Curved, Making, 154
—— ——, Gilding and Embossing, 96, 97
—— ——, Silvering, 139, 140
Silex for making Glass, 150
Silica for making Glass, 150
Silvering Sheet Glass, 139, 140
—— Speculum, 137–139
Size for Gilding Glass, 96
Soda Glass, 150, 152

Soda Glass, Glass-pots for, 153
—— ——, Tubes of, 26
Spectacle Frames, Fitting Lenses into, 147–149
—— Lens, Ascertaining Focus of, 147
—— ——, Grinding Edges of, 149
—— ——, Shanks for Nibbling, 149
Specula, Telescope, Hand-working of, 113–139 (for details, see Speculum, below)
Speculum, Figuring, 128
——, Foucault Shadow Test for, 130–136
——, Pitch Pads for Polishing, 126–128
——, Polishing, 125–130
——, Silvering, 137–139
——, Testing Focal Length of, 125
——, Working, Convex Tool used in, 114
—— ——, Curve Gauge used in, 116, 119
—— ——, Direction of Strokes for, 123
—— ——, Draper's Table of Emery Grades for, 121
—— ——, Emery used in, 120–122
—— ——, Glass Discs for, 117
—— ——, Hone Square Tool used in, 114
—— ——, Materials for, 116
—— ——, Old Method of, 113, 114
—— ——, Pitch used in, 122–126
—— ——, Ross's Table of Emery Grades for, 121
—— ——, Rouge used in, 122
—— ——, Sand used in, 120
Spheroid, Oblate, 134–136
Spherometer, 147
Spirit Blowpipe, 10–12
—— Lamp, 23, 24
—— —— Flame, Bending Tubes in, 32
Stand Blowpipe, 16
Steam Dipping Vat, 87, 88
Stiletto, 87, 91
Stirrers, Making, 38, 39

Table for Glass Blower, 18
—— Glass, White, Recipes for, 152
Tables of Emery Grades, 121
Telescope Specula, Hand-working of, 113–139 (For Details, see Speculum)
Test Glasses, Making, 79
Testing Focal Length of Spectacle Lens, 147
—— —— —— —— Speculum, 125
—— Lenses, 145–147

Testing Speculum by Foucault Shadow Method, 130–136
Test-tube, Finishing Mouth of, 39, 40
——, Making, 34–38
——, Re-making Mouth of, 97
——, Re-sealing, 99
Thermometer Bulb, Blowing, 62
Thistle Funnel, Making, 75–78, 102
Tin Drill-bits, 108
Tobacco Pipes, Glass, 81–84
Tools, Diamond-pointed, for Working Glass in Lathe, 144
—— for Fitting in Spectacle Lenses, 147
Triangular Tool for finishing Mouths of Tubes, 40
Tube Drills for Glass, 105, 107, 108
—— Glass, Peligot's Bohemian, 152
Tubes, Absorption, 60
——, Bending, 29–32
——, Bulbs penetrated by, 67–71
——, Cutting, 28, 29, 39, 97, 98, 99
——, Drawing down, 54
——, File for Cutting, 26
——, Forming Bulb on Centre of, 57, 58
——, Forming several Bulbs on, 59–60
——, Four-way, Making, 44–48
——, Gallenkamp's Vacuum, 85
——, Joining large, to small ones, 42
——, ——, to Bulbs, 65
——, ——, together, 40–48
——, Sealing, 34–38
——, Test (see Test Tubes)
——, Three-way, Making, 44–47
——, Tools for forming Lips on, 26
——, U-shaped, 32, 33
——, Vacuum, 73, 85
——, Various kinds of, 26
Turning Glass in Lathe, 141–144

U-tubes, Making, 32, 33

Vacuum Tubes, Gallenkamp's, 85
—— ——, Making, 73
Vat, Steam Dipping, 87, 88

Water Air-pumps, 73
White Aciding Etched Glass, 93
Window Glass, 151, 152
Wine Glasses, Etching, 87–95
—— ——, Making, 78, 79
Wire for Riveting Glass, 109
Wires, Sealing Platinum, within Bulb, 73–75

Yellow Glass, 153

www.ingramcontent.com/pod-product-compliance
Lightning Source LLC
Chambersburg PA
CBHW011951150426
43195CB00018B/2887